Paths to Property

Approaches to Institutional Change in
International Development

Paths to Property
Approaches to Institutional Change in
International Development

KAROL BOUDREAUX & PAUL DRAGOS ALIGICA

FOREWORD BY PETER J. BOETTKE

The Institute of Economic Affairs

First published in Great Britain in 2007 by
The Institute of Economic Affairs
2 Lord North Street
Westminster
London SW1P 3LB
in association with Profile Books Ltd

The mission of the Institute of Economic Affairs is to improve public understanding of the fundamental institutions of a free society, by analysing and expounding the role of markets in solving economic and social problems.

Copyright © The Institute of Economic Affairs 2007

The moral right of the authors has been asserted.

All rights reserved. Without limiting the rights under copyright reserved above, no part of this publication may be reproduced, stored or introduced into a retrieval system, or transmitted, in any form or by any means (electronic, mechanical, photocopying, recording or otherwise), without the prior written permission of both the copyright owner and the publisher of this book.

A CIP catalogue record for this book is available from the British Library.

ISBN 978 0 255 36582 6

Many IEA publications are translated into languages other than English or are reprinted. Permission to translate or to reprint should be sought from the Director General at the address above.

Typeset in Stone by MacGuru Ltd
info@macguru.org.uk

Printed and bound in Great Britain by Hobbs the Printers

Cover photograph: The house (at right of picture) shows how shacks (such as the one at left of picture) are being replaced in South Africa as property rights become properly defined and tradable.

CONTENTS

The authors   7
Foreword by Peter J. Boettke   9
Acknowledgements   14
Summary   15
Figures and boxes   17
Preface by Richard Wellings   18

1 Introduction   23

2 Institutional policy and economic development   27
Institutions and economic theory   27
Property rights and economic growth   30
Creating effective institutions   35

3 Property rights and institutional complexity   38
The legal perspective on property rights   40
Property rights as social institutions   41
The economics of property rights   42
Enforcement and social norms   46
Criticisms of the evolutionary approach   47
Social capital and property rights   48

4	**Paths to the creation of property rights**	52
5	**Legislation and creation by fiat**	55
	The Samburus in Kenya	56
	Examples of legislation	57
	Wildlife management in Namibia	57
	Property titling in South Africa	60
6	**The evolutionary path**	71
	The evolution of property rights in Plateau, Nigeria	72
	Land ownership and cocoa production in western Ghana	76
	Individualisation and formalisation	78
7	**Summing up: fiat and evolution**	80
8	**An intellectual toolbox for the creation of property rights**	84
	The process view of property-rights systems	85
	The interplay of the formal and informal	90
	Incentives, costs and the critical role of economic thresholds	91
	Property-rights technology – the pivot of the property-rights system	93
	The crucial empirical content, relevant rules and the danger of 'slogan words'	97
9	**Conclusions**	100
	References	103
	About the IEA	112

THE AUTHORS

Karol Boudreaux

Karol Boudreaux is a Senior Research Fellow at the Mercatus Center and the lead researcher for Enterprise Africa! She also teaches law and international development at George Mason University. Before joining the Mercatus Center, she was assistant dean at George Mason University's School of Law. Ms Boudreaux is also a member of the Working Group on Property Rights of the UN's Legal Empowerment of the Poor Commission. Her main areas of interest include property rights and development, human rights and international law. The current focus of her research is contemporary Africa and the ways in which particular institutional arrangements have either helped or hindered human flourishing and economic development on the continent. Ms Boudreaux earned her BA in English literature from Rutgers University (Douglass College) and her JD from the University of Virginia's School of Law.

Paul Dragos Aligica

Paul Dragos Aligica is a Senior Research Fellow at the Mercatus Center and an Adjunct Fellow at the Hudson Institute. He has written on institutional change theories and strategies, international development issues and the political economy of transition and reform processes. In addition to his academic work, he has served as an expert for large international consulting firms and as an adviser or project partner for organisations such as the United Nations Development Programme and the United States Agency for International Development. Dr Aligica earned his PhD in political science from Indiana University, Bloomington. He also earned a PhD in economics from the Academy of Economic Studies in Bucharest and a PhD in sociology from the University of Bucharest.

FOREWORD

Adam Smith, in his notebooks, which would eventually contribute to *The Wealth of Nations*, wrote that: 'Little else is requisite to carry a state to the highest degree of opulence from the lowest barbarism, but peace, easy taxes and a tolerable administration of justice' (1976: xl). However sensible Smith's policy prescription is, he takes for granted in this passage the foundational institutions that produce a social order characterised by peace and justice. Fortunately, Smith's good friend David Hume, in his *A Treatise of Human Nature*, explicitly stated what those foundational institutions were. Stability of possession, transference by consent and the performance of promises provide the foundation of a peaceful social order; in their absence human society is impossible. 'Society is absolutely necessary for the well-being of men; and these are as necessary to the support of society' (1978: 526).

In *Paths to Property: Approaches to Institutional Change in International Development*, Karol Boudreaux and Paul Aligica tackle the question of the establishment of a private property rights regime in countries where property rights were previously collectivised, severely attenuate or ill defined and poorly defended. In short, their work is focused on those regions of the world where economic development has been lacking. In many of these countries the people are forced to live in horrific conditions of poverty and political tyranny. While they try to understand the transition to private property rights, Boudreaux and Aligica avoid slogans and quick-fix answers. In fact, they argue that while we might have very detailed knowledge of how the market economy can mobilise the energies of the people to realise the gains from exchange and create wealth within a system of private property rights, we have very little knowledge about how to design, create and secure such a regime of private property in the countries that need property rights the most, namely the underdeveloped economies of Africa and the transitioning former socialist economies.

In many significant respects the only path to reform is an indigenous one. Institutional change cannot be engineered from afar; and there is no one-size-fits-all prescription for development. On the other hand, while there are many ways for people to live, there are only a few ways for them to live peacefully and prosperously. And those few are all organised around a set of fundamental institutions that are nested within each other, with the most fundamental being the right to private property (stability of possession), freedom of contract (transfer by consent) and honest commercial dealings (promise-keeping).

As Boudreaux and Aligica show, countries that find their way to clearly defining and enforcing property rights realise the benefits of economic growth and development, while those that are unable to make that transition continue to suffer. But the authors go beyond simply documenting this experience in the modern history of development. They want to help provide methods to ease the path to property, and thus prosperity and peaceful social cooperation. They discuss recent history in Africa, China and Russia. In the process, they discuss not only the problems of the 'tragedy of the commons', when property rights are ill defined or collectivised, but also the 'tragedy of the anti-commons', when property rights are too fragmented by policy design and thus generate unintended and undesirable consequences on the path to property.

Functional property rights regimes exist within a complex web of institutions, including the rules of acquisition, transfer and use, as well as the mechanisms of enforcement and dispute resolution, all embedded within a support system of norms, values and beliefs. In an economy, the operating property rights regime is the by-product of the action of 'property rights entrepreneurs' (who are always within a particular context of time and space) and longer-term evolutionary processes that govern social intercourse. From a strict economic perspective, property rights entrepreneurs will define and enforce property rights when the benefits of having a well-defined system outweigh the costs of creating such a system. This act of creation often takes place at the local level, but it could in theory be initiated at higher levels of government – including the legislature. Some mix of Coase and Hayek helps us work towards an answer. Faced with conflicts of resource use and interpretation of who owns what, we seek to rely on norms and conventions to get the initial 'ownership' endowment, and then we rely on exchange processes to negotiate away the conflict. If negotiations break down because of continuing confusion over ownership, then we seek resolution through clarification of ownership rights with the courts. A judge will adjudicate our case and clarify the property rights structure, which in turn will enable us to negotiate away any conflicts. If adjudication is unable to fix our problems, then perhaps the legislature might provide some relief. Boudreaux and Aligica provide some evidence from Africa that while legislation can create property rights quickly and unequivocally, it can also introduce conflicts and controversy over the property rights structure.

So the simple Coasean formula for resolving disputes over resource use – negotiate, adjudicate, legislate – has its limitations. Only when the informal norms, customs, habits and beliefs align with the newly established formal institutions of property, contract and consent will the positive impact of the property rights structure be realised.

When property rights are so embedded in an environment where they 'stick', the path to property leads to the path to prosperity in short order. Property rights provide the foundation for the market economy. Without private property rights there would be no exchange, and without exchange there would be no prices, and without prices there would be no rational accounting based on profit and loss statements. The three Ps of property, prices and profit/loss provide within a dynamic economy the three Is of incentives, information and innovation. High-powered incentives, the mobilisation and utilisation of dispersed information, and the constant striving to innovate and find lower-cost ways to produce existing goods and services, as well as to discover new goods and services that others desire more highly, are what defines a thriving economic system. As stated earlier, the path to property paves the way for the path to prosperity.

Hopefully for the millions of poor souls still struggling in conditions of severe poverty the international development policy community will listen to Boudreaux and Aligica, and learn how to find the most effective path to property for each of the countries the agencies are seeking to help. It is not foreign aid which will help these countries; and foreign aid will be redundant if they find the way to private property, freedom of contract and promise-keeping, because the opportunities for mutually beneficial exchange and wealth creation will be plentiful. Poverty will finally become a thing of the past rather than a trap from which they cannot seem to escape.

PETER J. BOETTKE
BB&T Professor for the Study of Capitalism at the Mercatus Center and
University Professor, Department of Economics,
George Mason University, Fairfax, Virginia
September 2007

The views expressed in this monograph are, as in all IEA publications, those of the authors and not those of the Institute (which has no corporate view), its managing trustees, Academic Advisory Council members or senior staff.

ACKNOWLEDGEMENTS

The IEA would like to acknowledge a generous grant from the Templeton Foundation which helped finance the research and its publication.

SUMMARY

- Economic development requires the creation of sound political and legal institutions – in particular, secure and functional property rights.
- Among policy-makers there is still widespread ignorance about how to design, create and secure functional property rights systems in the developing world. Detailed institutional analysis may therefore be more productive than engaging in the old 'nationalisation' versus 'privatisation' debate.
- Successful programmes of property rights reform recognise the complexity and uniqueness of existing property environments. Each individual context calls for a discrete response. Quick-fix, universal solutions are likely to fail.
- Because there is no unique solution to fit all cases, one needs to think of property rights policy as a strategic process, not a blueprint-based social engineering undertaking.
- The available strategies of property rights creation are defined by the various combinations of two basic paths: evolutionary (spontaneous, bottom-up) and legislative (top-down, fiat).
- Understanding whether or not the de facto property environment matches or tracks de jure rules is crucial. Caution against over-reliance on fiat and legislation should be paralleled by balanced and realistic expectations regarding the power and limits of the evolutionary approach.

- Property rights could hardly exist without institutional and technological means of defining, monitoring and enforcing them. 'Property-rights technologies' are a key consideration in any strategy of creating property rights.
- Property rights have an economic basis. There are economic thresholds beyond which it makes economic sense to introduce property rights and thresholds under which costs hinder the emergence of specific property arrangements.
- A process view of property rights reform shifts the attention from the creation of a static configuration of rules and laws to the creation of a flexible and resilient system which can adapt to changes in costs, technologies and social circumstances.
- Expectations regarding property-rights-based development policies are high and rising. It is therefore essential that implementation strategies take adequate account of their cultural and institutional contexts. Disappointing outcomes resulting from defective implementation may lead eventually to the dismissal of the idea that robust property-rights systems are essential for economic growth.

FIGURES AND BOXES

Figure 1	Economic freedom and per capita GDP	32
Box 1	Property rights in Botswana	44
Box 2	Property rights in China	65
Box 3	Property rights in Russia	68

PREFACE

The late Peter Bauer (Lord Bauer of Market Ward) demonstrated that the economic results of foreign aid are negative. Yet almost forty years after the publication of his classic *Dissent on Development*, powerful coalitions of non-governmental organisations such as Make Poverty History continue to lobby Western governments to increase aid payments to developing countries. Accordingly, state expenditure on 'development assistance' has increased in recent years, as if decades of failure can be overturned by sending yet more money. In reality this means predatory governing elites will continue to be propped up by these aid payments. Continued social breakdown and aid dependency will be inevitable consequences of the burgeoning global welfare state.

The Enterprise Africa! project was undertaken to challenge the conventional wisdom that economic development can be brought about by a combination of state intervention and foreign assistance. This initiative, a joint venture involving the Mercatus Center at George Mason University, the Free Market Foundation of southern Africa and the Institute of Economic Affairs, has sought to examine alternative policies based on trade and entrepreneurship among individuals rather than economic planning by government diktat. A team of researchers led by Karol Boudreaux (one of the authors of this monograph) travelled through sub-Saharan

Africa over a two-year period conducting detailed research on the role of local entrepreneurs and markets in overcoming poverty. They looked at coffee production in Rwanda, mobile phones in Botswana, natural resources in Namibia and taxis in South Africa – to list just some of the case studies. The results are very encouraging.

The researchers have shown that private enterprise has played a pivotal role in raising living standards in many different parts of Africa. Indeed, entrepreneurs have often been able to bring about improvements despite facing predatory governments and political instability. The team have published their findings in the *Mercatus Policy Series*, and in a symposium on 'Enterprise Solutions to Poverty in Africa' in the June 2007 issue of *Economic Affairs*. The research has also been disseminated through more than two dozen newspaper articles. In addition, several meetings have been held with academics, politicians and representatives of aid organisations. As a result it is hoped that the development establishment will become more receptive to measures that facilitate trade and entrepreneurship and less focused on programmes based on foreign aid, thereby avoiding the devastating policy mistakes of the twentieth century.

While the Enterprise Africa! studies have shown that Africa's entrepreneurs are making an important contribution to the alleviation of poverty on that continent, it is clear that their activities are hampered by the shortcomings of their governments. In particular, the absence in many countries of secure and transferable property rights acts as a significant deterrent to medium- and long-term investment. Entrepreneurs are therefore likely to remain small-scale rather than developing into the tycoons that drove forward industrialisation, first in Europe and North America, and later in the Far East. This monograph therefore addresses the question of how best to create or reform property rights systems in developing countries. Although solutions may usefully be informed by political and economic theory, the authors draw on the project's detailed case studies to suggest that property-rights policies are more likely to succeed when they develop gradually and are tailored to local norms and circumstances rather than imposed from above by governments and supranational institutions. This is an important conclusion which cuts across conventional ideological divisions and shows the practical policy value of the Enterprise Africa! initiative.

DR RICHARD WELLINGS
Deputy Editorial Director,
Institute of Economic Affairs
September 2007

Paths to Property

Approaches to Institutional Change in International Development

1 INTRODUCTION

Much recent work in economics and political science focuses on the role institutions play in creating social order and promoting or hindering economic development. A significant part of this interest was triggered by a startling reality: despite the transfer of more than a trillion dollars in development aid from the developed to the developing world over the last several decades, absolute poverty persists. Many countries, particularly in Africa, are still desperately poor – indeed, some are poorer today than they were in the 1970s. The traditional approaches to international development have failed. While a host of notable voices, under the spell of old thinking, still issue loud calls for increases in aid to the developing world, others, drawing on recent advances in economic and political theory, look to the institutional environment and alternative strategies of institutional change for more robust and constructive answers to the riddle of international development.

This study examines the challenges posed by one of these institutions – property rights. The academic literature suggests that secure rights to property provide an important foundation for an economically vibrant society. The problem of how best to implement policies that create and secure these rights therefore becomes an important practical challenge for both the international development community and officials in the developing world. Put another way, what are the most effective reform strategies aimed at property rights creation and preservation? What are the most fruitful approaches to the creation of an institutional environment conducive to efficient and adaptive property rights arrangements? How can we 'get the institutions right'?

Drawing mainly on examples from sub-Saharan Africa, this study explores the avenues of property rights creation and change. The institutional environment in African countries is both rich and challenging, providing paradigmatic examples of the ways in which property rights have developed and changed over time in response to local needs and external intervention. Two basic ideal types will be employed to conceptualise the paths to the creation of property rights: (1) via decentralised evolutionary transformation; and (2) via centralised legislative intervention. Either path may, in particular circumstances, lead to positive, efficient and freedom-enhancing changes. In other cases, either path may lead to negative changes that limit freedom and hamper economic development. In some situations it will be beneficial to formalise property rights while in other situations formalising these rights will create opportunities for elites to capture much of the value of the formalised property. Similarly, in some cases customary law will provide relative security of property rights, in large part because customary law reflects social norms and belief systems. Customary law may also, however, marginalise minority groups, outsiders and women. Identifying which path to follow in the search for secure property rights is a daunting challenge.

We argue that, despite the strong temptation to search for universal or 'one-size-fits-all' solutions, there is no single formula for the creation of secure property rights (Deininger, 2003; Lund et al., 2006: 3). Rather, the path chosen in a given situation will require a strong knowledge of the specific institutional environment, stakeholders' interests and local culture, as well as an astute application of strategic rationality. While the proposition that secure rights to property will further economic development is uncontroversial, our study focuses on the insight that there is no one 'correct' way to create secure property rights. We argue that policy change that leads to secure property rights is a dynamic process and therefore policymakers who wish to amend the property-rights environment must be alert to the fluid and complex nature of the policy process. We offer several basic elements of an intellectual toolbox that highlight common pitfalls that may frustrate policy reform. We also identify several strategic issues to be considered when contemplating change to the property-rights environment. It is our contention that by embracing the specific nature of property environments, the conceptual space defining the policy programme of property rights creation will become better attuned to the practical challenges of the international development agenda.

Our study should be seen as a contribution to what in the policy evaluation literature is called the 'programme theory' element (or phase) of a policy process (Rossi, 2004; Bickman, 1987), and more specifically to its implementation dimension. As Rossi, one of the key authors in the field, puts it, 'program theory has been described and used under various names' (i.e. conceptual map, and action theory) but 'there is no general consensus about how best to describe a program's theory' (Rossi, 2004: 136). Yet the essence of the idea is simple: it refers to the conceptual space surrounding a specific policy programme or policy agenda and it consists of notions, theories, models, lessons learned and various 'know-how' elements in various stages of aggregation and conceptualisation. As such, 'it is the foundation on which every program rests'. A programme's theory, adds Rossi, 'can be a good one, in which case it represents the "know-how" necessary for the program to attain the desired results, or it can be a poor one that would not produce the intended effects even if implemented well' (ibid.: 134–6).

For 'programme theory' to be assessed and improved, however, it must first be explored and expressed as clearly as possible. The ongoing effort of adjustment between, on the one hand, theory and, on the other hand, policy and practice always requires a periodic reconsideration of 'programme theory'. Seen from this perspective, our study, anchored on both sides of the theory–policy divide, is an instantiation of a standard practice: the practice of taking stock of a policy-relevant issue and its conceptual wrapping, and of discussing it by looking both backward and forward at some of the most important lessons learned and challenges ahead. It is an unassuming contribution, yet one that is always indispensable for the advancement of any policy agenda.

2 INSTITUTIONAL POLICY AND ECONOMIC DEVELOPMENT

Institutions and economic theory

Over the past three decades economists have made a strong, sustained case for the tenet that economic development is closely correlated with the strength or weakness of institutional arrangements (North and Thomas, 1973; North, 1990, 1989; Rodrik et al., 2004; Weingast, 1995). In his 1993 Nobel Prize speech Douglass North said: 'Institutions form the incentive structure of a society and the political and economic institutions, in consequence, are the underlying determinant of economic performance.' A direct implication of this is the idea that the economic and political performance of a society is not primarily determined by the availability of resources and related constraints but by institutional successes or failures (Olson, 1982; Ostrom, 1993; Pipes, 1999).

The applied or policy-level corollary of these conclusions is that economic development strategies should be seen as a combination of two types of approaches: those aiming to optimise the economic processes within existing institutional arrangements and those aiming to transform (or reconstruct) the existing institutional framework in ways that would create the conditions for growth-generating economic processes. The first approach has been at the core of economic policy since World War II. Its strategy is a matter of manipulating policy 'instruments' within given 'systemic parameters'. A policy had *targets* (that is, goals or desired values of endogenous variables derived from the preferences of policymakers) and the targets were reached by applying *instruments* (exogenous variables controlled by policymakers). This so-called *quantitative policy* model prescribed what target values were attainable and how they could be attained (Hansen, 1963: 7; Eggertsson, 1997: 63). In other words, this strategy takes as given the structure of the economic system and manipulates existing economic relationships towards a specific target.

The other type of strategy is different. Institutional or *structural policy* seeks to change the structure of the system. If, in the case of quantitative policy, the (immediate) goal is to achieve a new value for a target variable then, in the case of qualitative policy, the objective is to add new variables and to create a new relationship between instruments and targets (Eggertsson, 1997: 64).

Until recently mainstream economic theory was relevant primarily for quantitative policy. According to this view, the economic system was exogenous and in most cases reduced to several primitive parameters. The approach seemed to have universal validity as most of its applications were used in the case of the stable, Western system (although its relevance had been a matter of debate even in that case). On the other hand, unlike quantitative policy, institutional or structural policy could not be employed effectively without a theory of institutions and institutional change (North, 1997: 14–16; Eggertsson, 1997: 63). This type of strategy required a different approach based on a deeper understanding of the social, cultural and historical context of economic policy decision-making. Moreover, in most cases those cultural, social and institutional elements were not the context but part and parcel of policymaking.

One of the consequences of the dichotomy created by the conceptual separation between structural policy and quantitative policy was that most economists specialised in quantitative policy. Structural policy issues were relegated to what was increasingly seen as the periphery of the field: development economics, economic history and comparative economic systems. And even there they were more or less neglected. As Hayek (1974) put it, 'while in the physical sciences the investigator will be able to measure what, on the basis of a prima facie theory, he thinks important, in the social sciences often that is treated as important which happens to be accessible to measurement'. This left most economists unprepared to deal with the profound structural policy issues posed by the international development challenge. In policy area after policy area the development experience exposed the inability of the field to identify or anticipate crucial problems and to articulate credible solutions. And thus, failure after failure piled up in the practice of international development (Easterly, 2003). Out of that, a series of very important lessons emerged and, in a sense, the new institutionalism may be seen as an attempt to synthesise and organise these lessons.

The institutionalist message is clear: in order to generate economic performance one needs to transform the institutional framework or architecture of a social system in a specific direction. Systems that effectively combine institutions in ways that provide for relatively low transaction costs, that generate voluntary exchange, reduce uncertainty, capture and distribute relevant information, encourage innovation, increase coordination and cooperation and control conflict, are better able to create the conditions for sustained economic growth. While we now recognise that institutions matter, there is also a perception that, in a sense, some institutional arrangements are foundational or more basic than others. And in this respect special attention has been given to the institution of property rights.

Property rights and economic growth

Authors such as Nobel laureates Ronald Coase and Douglass North have insisted on the importance of well-specified, secure rights to property for economic growth. In their work they open up an entirely new research programme by elaborating and explaining the link between property rights, transaction costs and economic performance. Trade, economic exchange and property rights are facets of the same social process leading to economic development. If one does not hold secure rights to a piece of property – personal property, real property, tangible or intangible property – there is little opportunity for voluntary exchange. There may be opportunities for theft or plunder, but not for mutually beneficial trading relations leading to the productive allocation of social resources. Trade, in turn, drives economic growth so long as the institutional framework within which traders operate provides for relatively low transaction and production costs 'in a world of specialization and division of labor' (North, 1990: 98). Property rights are one of the institutions that help to lower the costs of transacting and which promote cooperative behaviour, allowing individuals or organisations to gain from trade. When property rights are secure, individuals have stronger incentives to seek profits, to enter into contracts and to resolve disputes. In addition, with secure property rights people are more likely to invest in both physical and human capital (Libecap, 2000; Deininger, 2003).

Economic growth rates are higher and people are wealthier in nations where property rights are secure and where the government uses its powers of public expropriation only sparingly. Recent research suggests a strong positive relation between a country's level of economic development and the security of property rights in that country (Knack and Keefer, 1995; Acemoglu et al., 2001; Zak, 2002; Gradstein, 2004). Wealthier societies are more likely than poorer ones to enforce property rights, providing more security to rights-holders. Gradstein argues that public enforcement of property rights takes place in wealthier countries where individuals willingly bear the burden of enforcement costs. Improved enforcement 'causes economic growth, thus perpetuating the willingness to secure property rights'. The result, he says, is a bifurcated world: one in which property rights are protected and incomes are high and the other where there is minimal public enforcement of property rights coupled with low incomes (Gradstein, 2004: 2).

Evidence of this relationship is seen in reports such as the *Index of Economic Freedom*, produced annually since 1995 by the Heritage Foundation and the *Wall Street Journal* in association with other think tanks such as the IEA. This index ranks countries numerically to determine which are the most economically free. The ranking measures ten economic freedoms, one of which is property rights. These measures are weighted equally and scored on a 1–100 scale with 100 representing an environment or policies conducive to maximum economic freedom. Property rights are defined as 'an assessment of the ability of individuals to accumulate private property, secured by clear laws that are fully enforced by the state'.

Results for 2007 show that the ten countries that ranked highest in the world in terms of economic freedom all received

Figure 1 **Economic freedom and per capita GDP**

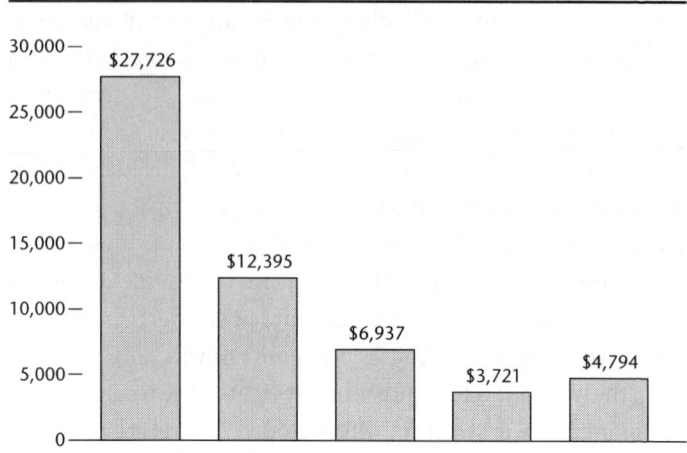

Source: 2007 *Index of Economic Freedom*

scores of 90 for their property-rights environment. Wealthy countries have the highest levels of property-rights protection. They do more to enforce these rights and to ensure that people are able to benefit from the creative use of property. The *Index* notes that the freest countries 'have twice the average per capita income of the second quintile of countries and over five times the average income of the fifth quintile of countries'. This relationship is illustrated in Figure 1, from the 2007 *Index*.

Compare these results with those for sub-Saharan Africa (SSA). According to the *Index*, SSA is the poorest region of the world with an average GDP per capita of $1,984 in 2006. This income level is one tenth that of the average income in the Americas and Europe (*Index of Economic Freedom*: 70). The average economic freedom score for SSA countries is 54.7, as compared with a world average of 60.6. The *Index* notes: 'Sub-Saharan Africa is also ranked last in seven of the 10 economic freedom categories and performs especially poorly in terms of property rights, freedom from corruption, and business freedom' (ibid.: 72). SSA countries score an average of 34 in property-rights protection, as compared with an average score of 61.7 for European countries and 48.5 for the Americas. No country in SSA scores higher than 70 out of 100 and half of the countries score just 30 out of 100 in property-rights protection. Among the lowest-scoring is Zimbabwe, a country that has experienced severe economic contraction over the past five years. Zimbabwe's property-rights measure in 2007 was a mere 10 out of 100. With such limited protection of property rights and limited governmental abilities to provide security and to enforce rights, the people of SSA face debilitating constraints in trade. In cases such as Zimbabwe, they also face severe insecurity when the government attempts to intimidate voters by demolishing the housing of the poor and powerless.

Results from the *Index* track those from other indices, including the Economic Freedom of the World rankings and the new International Property Rights Index. In their 2006 *Economic Freedom of the World* report, Gwartney, Lawson and Easterly point out that nations in the top quartile of economic freedom have an average per capita GDP of $24,402 compared with $2,998 for countries in the bottom quartile. Countries in the bottom quartile have negative economic growth rates of −0.2 per cent. Of the ten least free countries in the world, seven are in Africa. The majority of nations in the bottom quartile are in Africa.

The 2007 *International Property Rights Index* ranks 70 countries in terms of protection of physical and intellectual property.

Rankings are on a 0 (weakest level of protection) to 10 (strongest level of protection) basis. In this first iteration few African countries are ranked. Of those that are, three rank in the second quartile: South Africa, Tunisia and Mauritius. Malawi, Egypt and Tanzania are ranked in the third quartile and Kenya, Nigeria and Ethiopia are ranked in the bottom quartile. The average GDP per capita for countries in the second quartile is $15,679; for those in the third quartile it is $7,665 and for those in the bottom quartile $4,294. Citizens in countries in the top quartile have an average GDP per capita of $32,994, which is seven times greater than that of citizens in the bottom quartile. As with the *Index of Economic Freedom* and the *Economic Freedom of the World* rankings, a 'positively sloped trend line indicates that countries with stronger property rights protection enjoy a higher per capita income than countries at the low end of the IPRI rating' (IPRI, 2007: 31). The report notes this is a trend, not an unambiguously proven causality (ibid.).

In a similar vein, authors such Boettke et al. (2004) and Anderson and Hill (2003) emphasise that if entrepreneurship is the driver of economic change and development, the basic relationship between entrepreneurial behaviour and property rights is crucial for our understanding of economic development. Entrepreneurship is an avenue for using property in potentially valuable ways and for keeping economies dynamic. This dynamism would be quashed, however, if entrepreneurs were unable to use property to create value. Wealth creation depends upon an institutional environment that provides individuals with secure rights to use and transfer property and which allows for and encourages entrepreneurship.

Creating effective institutions

The robust finding that property rights are among the most important institutions in terms of economic development is counterbalanced by the observation that creating effective institutions has proved to be extremely challenging. Our knowledge of how to design, create and secure functional property-rights systems in those areas and societies that need them most, the developing world, is incomplete. Economic indices, such as those mentioned above and the World Bank's *Doing Business* report, provide information about the relative strength or weakness of property rights in different nations.[1] These indices are helpful in highlighting problem areas such as the length of time it takes to register property or the lack of an independent judiciary. They can guide local officials and/or development experts who seek to identify the steps that should be taken to improve property rights in a given environment. Yet indices will take reformers only so far.

Institutional policies and strategies need more than just a mere general diagnosis based on statistical data points or generalisations constructed by academic researchers. Changing, adjusting or creating institutions are complex processes that depend on a large number of conditions and causes, specific to each case and context. As Deininger notes:

> In view of the wide variation of conditions across countries, it is impossible to implement 'patent recipes' without an awareness of local conditions. Doing so can result in ad hoc interventions that can have serious negative impacts. For example, if the legal basis is inadequate, modernizing

---

[1] The 2007 *Index of Economic Freedom* can be accessed at *www.heritage.org/index/*. The *Economic Freedom of the World* report is found at *www.freetheworld.com/release.html*. See www.doingbusiness.org for the World Bank's reports and data.

> land administration institutions and land records may be of doubtful value. (Deininger, 2003: 179)

As this quote makes clear, institutions do not exist in a void; rather, they are strongly linked to each other. They form an interrelated system that evolves and adjusts in response to changes in the individual institutions. A change in an institutional component such as a property-rights arrangement usually implies changes in other, connected or related, institutions. In other words, embedded or nested institutional arrangements are the norm. Institutional change strategies aimed at generating economic development must therefore take into account the systemic nature of institutional arrangements.

The idea that institutions such as property rights are nested in other institutions and that they reciprocally define their functioning offers a very powerful framework for policy analysis and social change (USAID, 2007). The relationships between institutions and their mutual enforcement, or the possible frictions and tensions emerging when they clash or overlap, constitute an important reality to be taken into account by any institutional change initiative. Given this complexity, institutional change strategies or institutional design efforts should reject mechanical, formulaic approaches or the application of some allegedly universal solution. Rather, such interventions should take into account the institutional intricacies specific to each particular case, including contextual variables and the actions and beliefs of stakeholders. This suggests that institutional design and change are *processes* in which not only a systemic understanding is needed but also a prudent application of strategic rationality. Moreover, as with any strategic process, uncertainty abounds.

The remainder of the study explores some of the problems and challenges associated with the strategies and policy processes that may lead to the creation of property rights. For example, how does the reality of institutional complexity affect policies that seek to create or consolidate property rights? What are the conceptual lenses that help us to deal with the complexity of property-rights systems in the non-Western context? In the light of the institutionalist literature it has become apparent that the search for a formula or universal solution for property-rights arrangements is futile. At the same time, it is clear that the absence of such a formula should not immobilise the reform process. The very attempt to deal with these questions will put policymakers in a better position to understand what is involved in the process of creating property-rights systems in the developing world and thus better prepare them for practice.

3 PROPERTY RIGHTS AND INSTITUTIONAL COMPLEXITY

While general lessons remain relevant, it is absolutely essential that policymakers understand both the structural complexity and the de facto environment of property-rights systems. Adequate account must be taken of the variety of stakeholders involved and the broad institutional context that exists in a given place at a given time, together with the customs and social norms that apply to the sphere of property use and transfer. Property rights imply a complex web of interactions: of acquisition, transfer and use rules, enforcement and monitoring systems, identification and information-storage mechanisms (whether formal or informal), and dispute resolution procedures, all supported by a variety of norms, values and beliefs.

The intricacy of the property-rights phenomenon in its many contextually determined forms escapes a unique definition or conceptualisation. Accordingly, the various aspects of property rights have been approached and discussed in the literature from many different perspectives. Only when put together do these discussions offer something closer to a realistic image of the complexity of the property-rights phenomenon. Recognising and taking into account its multiple facets has important consequences for the way we approach the task of creating or restructuring property-rights systems, especially in the non-Western, developing world.

If policy reform generally is a dynamic process, so too is property-rights reform. Policy change to secure property rights will occur in discrete property environments, each of which will in all likelihood call for its own response. For instance, in African countries, property rights exist in an environment in which customary law dealing with land use and allocation typically coexists with statutory law and elements of colonial-era law, either common or civil. If nations are signatories to regional and international conventions that seek to protect property rights, further layers of rules are added. Any institutional reform may need to consider several levels of legal rules simultaneously or sequentially in addition to other concerns.

The reality of institutional complexity means it is essential to identify and understand which property rules obtain in particular situations and how the differing rules interact. As property rights are embedded in other institutions, a variety of other legal rules – rule-of-law issues, labour regulations, banking regulations, etc. – also often influence whether or not a property-rights reform will be 'successful'. In addition to formal legal rules, one must identify if and how customary law, social norms and belief systems regarding property affect the observation and enforcement of rules. For example, giving women the legal right to inherit property, via a statute or constitution, may not accomplish the goal of providing a thicker bundle of secure rights if customary law and/or social norms on the ground oppose this change.

In addition to identifying which rules and norms may affect property rights, it is also important to identify actual or potential drivers (blockers) of property change. For instance, who has something to gain or something to lose from the status quo or from changes in property-rights rules? Sometimes changes are instigated by property-rights entrepreneurs, who may risk sanctions in exchange for expected gains from shifting rules (Anderson and Hill, 2003: 120–24). In other cases, change may reflect a broader shift in social norms. Put somewhat differently, it is important to understand who demands and who supplies institutional change and why (Feeny, 1993). Moreover, it is necessary to understand how these 'drivers' of change add new layers of complexity to a property-rights problem.[1] Any intervention will sooner or later have to cope with the daunting diversity and intricacy exhibited by property rights and property-rights-associated social structures.

The following brief overview of some of the conceptual frameworks used in the study of property rights further illustrates the nature of the complexity of property environments. Property rights have, of course, a legal dimension but they also have economic, cultural and sociological dimensions. In order to create more secure rights to property, policymakers and practitioners would be well advised to take all these aspects of property into consideration.

The legal perspective on property rights

A typical entry point when dealing with property rights is to see them from a legal perspective. Reference texts in law state that property rights are 'any type of right to specific property whether

---

[1] When changes to a property-rights environment reflect a broad social consensus – captured in custom and social norms – about how to allocate resources, these changes are more likely to be respected and enforced. When changes reflect narrow interests, however, and/or when they enrich local elites or political or business elites, the changes may well lead to conflict – even if, perhaps especially if, these changes are in the direction of increased individualisation.

it is personal or real property, tangible or intangible. [Property is] an aggregate of rights which are guaranteed and protected by the government ... That dominion or indefinite right of use or disposition which one may lawfully exercise over particular things or subjects'.[2] Lawyers, and many economists, use a 'bundle of sticks' analogy when discussing property rights – the rights are described as sticks in a bundle. Each right, or stick, is discrete and separable from the others. Taken together, or 'bundled', the sticks make up a substantial and sometimes very complex whole. When individuals are empowered to decide which sticks they wish to keep and which they wish to trade away or purchase, they have a broader authority or dominion over resources and increased opportunities to make profitable use of them. This does not mean, however, that rights to property should always be allocated to individuals. Individuals often choose to define some rights as collective rights because individual allocation is perceived to be too costly (Ostrom, 1990).

Property rights as social institutions

A somewhat broader definition and approach would be that property rights are the social institutions that define and limit the privileges individuals hold with regard to specific resources (Libecap, 1989: 1). Property rights typically develop and evolve in situations where a social consensus supports particular decisions regarding the allocation, use and transfer of resources. At times, of course, rights are created by fiat and may signal little social consensus. Rights may be formalised in legislation or regulation or they may be informal rules and norms. Either way, so long as

---

[2] *Black's Law Dictionary* (1993).

people respect the rules and the rules are enforced, both varieties of rights – formal and informal – work effectively. Nevertheless, the formal–informal dichotomy and the social mechanisms associated with it further complicate the ways in which we understand property rights arrangements.

The economics of property rights

Irrespective of their conceptualisation, one of the general lessons we have learned about property rights is that they are costly to create. This is an important consideration which introduces further complexity to property-rights systems. Efforts to create more secure property rights will involve a variety of costs: mapping the property-rights environment, clearly defining new rights, working with change agents (blockers) effectively, as well as implementation and enforcement. While scholars point to the costliness of defining and enforcing rights, reforms may not last if change agents are ignored or if the baseline property environment is not fully understood and mapped.

It is costly to create property rights but it can also be costly to transgress social norms related to property use. Transgressions can lead to a variety of sanctions: curses, ostracism, loss of reputation and penalties are just some examples. Thus bundles of rights bring with them bundles of social norms and costly social processes. A system of property rights is costly to create or modify because it requires that people devote time and effort to defining the extent and scope of the rights. They must specify who does or does not hold which rights and, importantly, they must enforce the rights against others.

Economists argue that people are willing to incur the expense of creating rights when the marginal benefits exceed the marginal costs involved (Libecap, 1989: 126–9). Benefits will normally exceed costs when a resource becomes scarcer. Scarcity will induce individuals to experiment with different property rules in an effort to find a system that improves their wellbeing by allowing them to capture more of the value of the resource. This evolutionary view of property is often interpreted as increasing the efficient allocation of scarce resources by channelling them to their highest-valued user. As discussed below, some scholars question this premise.

Sometimes property-rights entrepreneurs are individuals or small groups (for example, cattlemen in the American West who developed individualised rights over grazing land); at other times, a broader swath of society experiments with new rules. This experimentation can happen under any legal system: customary law, common or civil law, or with a statutory regime. As a general rule, the more specific a right is, the more expensive it will be to create and enforce. As resources become increasingly scarce and therefore more valuable, it will become increasingly worthwhile to go to the time and effort involved in creating more specific rights over those resources. For example, economist Harold Demsetz argued: 'the emergence of new property rights takes place in response to the desires of interacting persons for adjustment to new benefit–cost possibilities … property rights develop to internalize externalities when the gains of internalization become larger than the cost of internalization' (Demsetz, 1967: 350; Ault and Rutman, 1979: 163–82).

Box 1 Property rights in Botswana

Botswana has led the African continent in terms of consistent economic growth rates over the past 30 years. It maintained one of the world's highest economic growth rates from 1966 to 1991 – these rates were 6.1 per cent per annum and income during those years rose from less than $600 per capita to nearly $4,000 per capita. Other indicators of wellbeing, including literacy rates, access to healthcare and access to clean water, have also improved dramatically.

Much of this growth can be attributed to the wise and restrained use of revenues flowing from diamond mining. Another part of the answer may lie in the country's property-rights environment. The 1968 Tribal Land Act, which was amended in 1993, provides clear rules concerning the use, transfer and acquisition of communal lands (Dougan, 2004). Such clarity improves the security of property rights. Interestingly, the 1967 Mines and Minerals Act transferred rights to subsurface mineral wealth to the national government; previously, such rights were held by tribes. Unlike other African nations, however, and despite the nationalisation of diamond wealth, Botswana has largely avoided the 'resource curse' thanks to a strong institutional environment (Acemoglu et al., 2001).

Botswana has generally succeeded, where other African nations (most notably its next-door neighbour Zimbabwe) have failed, not only because of the natural resources but also as a result of its relatively healthy institutions. Restraints on spending, a rule of law, low levels of corruption and respect for certain classes of property were important determinants of its performance. In 2007, the *Index of Economic Freedom* ranked Botswana second in Africa, behind Mauritius.

While there has been important and sustained economic progress in the country since 1970, there are some reasons for concern. As Susan Anderson notes: '[a]n unintended consequence of the rapid development is that Botswana today is weighted with a huge and pervasive government. Macroeconomic data indicate a significant dependence upon government spending. Government expenditure accounts for over half of GDP, and over 65% of the total national revenue collected for that expenditure comes from state-owned enterprises, and government ownership of property. An estimated 43% of the labor force works in the public sector' (Anderson, 2005: 11).

In terms of its property-rights environment, Botswana protects investors' rights and does have an independent, if much overworked, judiciary, but there is also room for improvement. For example, the country does a relatively poor job of protecting the rights of women to inherit property. Although the country has *de jure* laws protecting women's rights to own, use and inherit land, courts often fail to enforce these rights, deferring instead to customary law and local norms. For example, women married under customary law are required to have their husband's approval to buy or sell property. With an extremely high incidence of HIV/Aids, many women in Botswana lose husbands, fathers and brothers to the disease but are unable to claim their rights to property. Land-grabbing is a problem, as widows are thrown off land so that other family members can stake claims.

In addition, starting in 1997, the government has been evicting indigenous bushmen (San) from their ancestral home areas in the Central Kalahari Game Reserve. The government claims the removal is necessary to preserve natural resources.

> It seems, however, that the area may also be a new source of diamonds. The San brought a class-action suit against the government for violating their constitutional rights. In December 2006 Botswana's High Court held that the government eviction was 'unlawful and unconstitutional'. Despite this, the government has not allowed the San to return to the reserve.

Enforcement and social norms

The corollaries of the above are many. Through them other facets of the complexity of property-rights arrangements are revealed. For instance, if scarcity and social norms are important, then one may conjecture that the degree to which change will be advantageous for new rights-holders depends, to a great extent, on two factors: (1) how property is divided if it becomes individualised; and (2) the effective enforcement of new rules. When allocations reflect the underlying social norms of a community these allocations are more likely to be respected and easily enforceable (Blocher, 2006: 173). Conversely, when they do not, new allocations may lead to conflict and difficulties enforcing rights. In addition, rule-of-law problems in many nations lead to insecure property rights. Collective-action problems and elite capture of resources may stymie the effective enforcement of evolving property-rights rules. Overcoming enforcement problems remains a major concern for those interested in developing secure property rights (Dam, 2006). But that is never a simple issue as it involves costs, incentives, social norms, customs, conflict management and monitoring mechanisms.

Criticisms of the evolutionary approach

For some scholars, the view of property rights as a social mechanism that evolves over time to promote efficiency through the reallocation of resources is too simplistic. Jean-Philippe Platteau, a land-tenure expert, argues that the empirical evidence does not fully support the evolutionary story. This theory cannot, he says, 'properly account for the oft-observed cases of chronic resource degradation', and he points to the overuse of their own grazing lands by Orma pastoralists in Kenya as just one example (Platteau, 2000: 74, 93).

Platteau also argues that the evolutionary story pays too little attention to the details of how communal property gets divided. The division process can be captured by either local elites or by government officials (Deininger, 2003: 9). In such cases, individualisation may not lead to efficiency-enhancing outcomes. This, he suggests, weakens the theoretical claims of the 'evolutionists'. Such examples illustrate how difficult it is to capture the property-rights cases using only one interpretive framework.

Evolutionary theorists have, however, pointed out that institutions *do not necessarily* evolve to meet the greatest good for the greatest number. North, for example, has argued: 'Institutions are not necessarily or even usually created to be socially efficient.' In some cases it may be better to see them as 'created to serve the interests of those with the bargaining power to create new rules'. In a world of zero transaction costs, 'bargaining strength does not affect the efficiency of outcomes; but in a world of positive transaction costs it does' (North, 1993).

Nonetheless, the concern that an evolutionary path to property expected to lead to a clarification and simplification can instead lead to inefficient allocations is very significant. One hopes that insofar as individual rights are tradeable, opportunities to trade will, over time, reduce inefficiencies and spread the gains from the property-rights creation, though such Coasean bargaining appears not to have worked well in post-Soviet Russia (Polishchuk and Savvateev, 2004). In cases such as these, policy interventions designed to limit predation or capture, and to move actors out of an evolutionary dead end may be required.

Social capital and property rights

It is important to note that some authors argue that a concentration on increased efficiency tends to obscure other aspects of the property-rights phenomenon that are at least as important as those revealed by the concept of efficiency. One of those neglected aspects is the important role that social capital plays in the evolution of property rights. Societies with relatively high levels of trust and social capital may have an easier time travelling the evolutionary path to property than societies with relatively low trust levels. In economic terms, higher levels of trust in a society mean it is less costly to transact with others; low-trust societies are high-transaction-cost societies (Putnam, 1994).

Markets and secure property rights may also promote the development of social capital by creating incentives for fairness, generosity and cooperation. In recent research in the developing world, a dozen anthropologists ran field experiments that involved giving one person a sum of money to share (or not) with another person. What the anthropologists discovered was surprising: those people who come from societies with higher degrees of market integration (expressed in terms of how frequently people engage in market transactions) tended to make more generous offers than did people who were less integrated into markets (Henrich et al., 2005).This research also notes that the sedentary groups studied also have higher 'payoffs to cooperation' than do the migratory or pastoralist groups. Sedentary groups tend to engage in more market transactions than do less settled groups. Thus, there is a correlation between groups that engage in higher levels of market exchange and the degree of fairness, generosity and cooperative behaviour that those groups demonstrate in their bargaining. This research challenges the notion that markets promote self-interested behaviour exclusively. As part of this body of research, anthropologist Jean Ensminger compared behaviour among two groups within the Orma community in Kenya. The Orma have traditionally been pastoralists, but some are now engaged in trade and earn a money wage. She discovered that traders and wage earners 'were more prone to engage in fair behavior than those more engaged in subsistence production' (Ensminger, 2004).

Property rights play a vital role in this equation. Giving more people secure bundles of property rights will provide them with greater opportunities to trade with others and to deepen their level of market integration. And if it is true that individuals who are more integrated into markets exhibit higher degrees of fairness, generosity and cooperative behaviour than do people who are less integrated, then property rights are an important part of the mechanism for generating pro-social behavioral norms and for lessening conflict.

Reputation, social norms and social exchange are issues anthropologists have been thinking and writing about with regard to property for more than a century. While some adopt a 'bundle of rights' approach and others focus on political or cultural aspects of property, all point out the complexity of the structure and dynamics of property-rights arrangements. Moreover, in their work they introduce the challenging problems of culture, power, values and perceptions. For example, anthropologist Katherine Verdery writes:

> Economists generally understand property as a means of regulating access to scarce resources and increasing their efficient use by assigning persons rights in them relative to other persons – a premise common to many political and legal scholars as well. Underlying this notion is the axiom, in my view highly questionable, that resources are naturally scarce *a priori* and that all we have to do is figure out how to get them and exclude others ... I hold, rather, that resources are *made* scarce within a given system of values and power relations ... Thus property as an institution often establishes scarcity rather than arising in response to it. (Verdery, 2003: 16).

Verdery (ibid.: 18) focuses on the role of property in signalling 'particular sets of social relationships – such as relations of use, of exclusive owning, and of obligation. Culturally speaking, property specifies what things have what kind of value and who counts as a person, and it then positions these in wider sets of social relations'. Property tells members of a particular community who belongs within the group and who is outside the group. In this view, property reflects in important ways not just one's place in society but also one's ability to enter into relationship with others. Verdery (ibid.: 19) suggests that property be treated as 'simultaneously a cultural system, a set of social relations, and an organization of power'.

To sum up, whether viewed through the lenses of lawyers, economists or anthropologists, property is a central organising feature of all societies and therefore one of the most complex social institutions. The variety of approaches and ways of conceptualising property rights and property-rights-related phenomena illuminates their complexity. Approaching the challenge of creating secure rights to property only through the avenue of legal rules and norms may mean overlooking important social or cultural issues that will affect implementation and enforcement. This complexity should not be seen as a merely analytical issue, or as a standard academic rhetorical device meant to cover our lack of understanding of social reality. If taken seriously as a statement about the factual challenges facing policymakers engaged in international development, it has very important implications for the practice of institutional change and international development.

4 PATHS TO THE CREATION OF PROPERTY RIGHTS

Once the challenge posed by the complexity of property rights and their environment is understood, one develops a clearer understanding of the dilemmas raised by the alternative strategies and policies aimed at property-rights creation. As has already been mentioned, in the international development community there is widespread acceptance of the idea that secure property rights contribute to poverty alleviation and to the creation of tradable assets that the poor can use to help improve their wellbeing. There is also an ongoing discussion of the role that property rights play in decentralising power and protecting individuals from various predations of elites. The important role property rights play in limiting arbitrary authority was highlighted by Hayek:

> The system of private property is the most important guarantee of freedom, not only for those who own property, but scarcely less for those who do not. It is only because the control of the means of production is divided among many people acting independently that nobody has complete power over us, that we as individuals can decide what to do with ourselves. If all the means of production were vested in a single hand, whether it be nominally that of 'society' as a whole or that of a dictator, whoever exercises this control has complete power over us. (Hayek, 1944: 103–4)

Secure property rights are widely viewed as the foundation

for more expansive trading relations, which in turn lead to higher levels of economic development. Thus, it is widely accepted that empowerment and development depend upon a secure property-rights environment (Boudreaux, 2005a: 15–16). Developing nations therefore have much to gain from creating and securing property rights. The problem then becomes one of practical application of these insights. The key question is how should property rights be generated, nurtured and maintained in a developing society? What is the best approach? What is the sequence of interactions that may lead to the creation or strengthening of this crucial institutional arrangement?

One way of approaching these questions is to use a framework inspired by institutional theory. We conceptualise the institutional change process in two basic ways: via evolution or gradual shifts in informal rules, and via legislation or shifts in formal rules and norms. By implication, there are two basic paths to the creation of property rights: via informal or evolutionary change and via formal or legislative change. In the first case the approach is either one of non-intervention or at most one of creating the conditions for the evolutionary process to take place. In the second, a direct and specific intervention is required. The two approaches could be seen as the end points of a spectrum of possible positions. If that is the case, then our strategies are defined by the various combinations of the two extreme ideal types: spontaneous, bottom-up, emergent evolutions; and top-down, precisely targeted, fiat interventions.

The real-life practice of policy and institutional design requires us to position our approaches on this continuum. To be effective our strategy has to be calibrated to the complexity and the specifics of each case. *There is no unique solution to fit all cases.*

In some instances, a more evolutionary approach may work; in others an intervention may be necessary to reset and restart the process, which may be blocked by various circumstantial or structural factors. The idea of one major move or sequences of moves that would create property rights and set into motion the development cycle overnight is naive. The quest for the miracle solution should therefore give way to the more mundane and difficult task of finding the proper approach that fits the configuration of the specific case of interest. Thus the question becomes: when to use and how to implement strategies that are closer to one end (ideal type) or another of the spectrum of possible alternatives.

The standard analytical narrative, which rationalises various stages and modes of emergence of property rights, implies no specific policy or strategy recommendation. This conclusion is confirmed by an in-depth look at concrete cases of both evolutionary and legislative property-rights changes. By drawing on examples from Africa, we illustrate how local examples of creating property rights contain lessons about what tends to work and what tends not to work on the ground.

5 LEGISLATION AND CREATION BY FIAT

The legislative path is considered a rapid course to the creation of property rights. Normally, it assumes a quick fix to a problem is possible. Indeed, many policies aimed at property rights were implemented under the assumption that property-rights systems could be created by fiat by a political or government body. It is true that, in many cases, governments create formal property via legislation that establishes new rights, or which codifies existing rights. At times, this path to property will operate effectively and individuals will benefit from increased security and thicker property-rights bundles. In some cases, when the economic mechanisms have been destroyed or have never existed in a functional form, the top-down legislative path is inescapable. Quite often, however, this path is subject to rent-seeking and capture by elites who use legislation to acquire and control property. Too often, legislation removes sticks from the bundle of property rights citizens hold, and this constricts trading opportunities, reduces the value of property and increases tenure insecurity.

Legislation can also create new rights that lead to conflict and controversy, particularly when small groups receive disproportionate benefits from the changes. In many cases a new property-rights structure is imposed over the old arrangements and is unable to endure. For example, in many developing countries traditional, local, informal systems of norms, institutions and customs are extremely resilient and resist formal, modernising legislation. This is not to say that the legislative fiat is universally doomed to fail in the developing world. But it means that the expectations one has from a pure fiat strategy – with no correlation and adaptation to contextual variables – should be appropriately calibrated.

The Samburus in Kenya

This problem may be illustrated by the case of the pastoralist Samburus, who live in Kenya. A small group of younger, literate Samburu men used the formal Kenyan legal system to acquire private rights over what had traditionally been communal land. This move was opposed by tribal elders, who saw the change in the property-rights environment as a violation of social norms and as an attempt to siphon valuable rents away from the group. In this case a legislative approach to creating property created conflict because social norms resisted the individualisation of property.

Lesorogol describes how this conflict was managed (2003: 531–42). The final outcome was an interesting compromise which involved the government providing each Samburu family in the settlement of Siambu with private rights to land. The young men got private land, but less than they had originally petitioned for; the elders pre-empted attempts by the younger men to take even larger parcels, which would have forced other community members on to less desirable land. One of the fascinating elements of this empirical example is how quickly social norms shifted to accept individualisation. Lesorogol says: 'Over the 15 years since the resolution of the land issue (in 1986) in Siambu, rhetoric regarding the virtues of private land ownership has developed with which virtually everyone, regardless of which side they were on during the conflict, concurs' (ibid.: 538). One common concern about the interplay between social norms and property rights is that norms change slowly and may impede the development of new rights. Lesorogol's work questions such assumptions.

Examples of legislation

Two recent examples of the legislative path to property provide useful lessons on the process of creating property rights by fiat: the devolution of property rights to manage wildlife and benefits from tourism to local groups in Namibia, and the policy in South Africa of providing titles to homes to residents in townships and other areas. In each case, the government has created new rights for citizens. These rights are relatively secure as both South Africa and Namibia have stable institutional environments that include stronger-than-average (as compared with other African nations) protection for property rights. In addition, these changes have support from a broad class of constituents, suggesting that they track nicely with underlying social norms. In each case, opportunities for predation are fairly limited. Neither policy change is perfect, but each seeks to accomplish important goals. We emphasise that these are only two cases – other examples would provide different lessons. Nevertheless, these efforts illustrate the complex nature of institutional change.

Wildlife management in Namibia

We begin with the case of Namibia. In the late 1960s, the government provided white farmers, who had freehold title to their land, with the legal right to manage wildlife found on their property and to benefit from associated tourism activities. This added another stick to the farmers' bundle of property rights – broadening their opportunities to engage in entrepreneurial activity and trade with others. The legislative change proved quite successful and farmers were able to diversify out of traditional ranching and into private game reserves.

After independence in 1990, the government conducted socio-economic surveys to identify the problems and concerns local black communities had in relation to the environment and conservation (Boudreaux, 2007).[1] Conservation efforts had been handled by the national government and local people had little involvement. Rights to use wildlife had been taken from them and many resorted to poaching. Land belonged to the government, not to local communities, though traditional authorities retained power to make decisions over who could use land and for what purpose. Under this system local people had few incentives to conserve wildlife because they received few benefits from this resource. In 1995, the government developed a policy for the creation of community-level conservancies and supplemented this with a second policy that would ensure the same rights to benefit from tourism on conservancy land that already applied on freehold land (Jones, 1999). These policies were the basis for the 1996 Natural Conservation Amendment Act, which amended the 1975 Nature Conservation Ordinance, and gave people living on communal land the same rights to manage wildlife as commercial farmers, so long as they grouped together into conservancies.

According to the legislation, conservancies must have a

---

1   For an extended discussion of community-based natural resource management in Namibia, see Boudreaux (2007).

defined border, a defined membership, a representative management committee and a legally recognised constitution that provides for a wildlife management strategy and the equitable distribution of benefits. Groups that meet these requirements may apply to the Ministry of Environment and Tourism to have their areas declared a conservancy. The legislation vests the legal right to manage and use wildlife, and to benefit from tourism, in communal areas in the hands of the management committee of the conservancy. Individual conservancy members do not hold these sticks, but they do hold voting rights, and therefore should be able to hold management committee members accountable for decision-making at annual general meetings. These legislative and policy changes created an institutional framework in Namibia that now provides local people with incentives to search for profitable ways to manage wildlife and develop tourist-related facilities within conservancies, either in partnership with more experienced tourism companies or on their own.

To date, the results in Namibia are quite encouraging. Over fifty conservancies have been formed. Only a small number are financially self-sufficient, but income levels from conservancy activities are rising at the same time that the amount of wildlife on conservancy land rises. Conservancy members now protect wildlife because they directly benefit from its presence. More animals are not always a welcome addition, however: more grazing animals mean that a conservancy has to devote land that could be used for grazing goats and cattle to wildlife. As most people living on conservancies raise livestock to earn a living, this is a significant trade-off, but conservancies nonetheless choose to divide their land to provide dedicated room for wildlife. More grazers also mean more predators, which, in turn, mean livestock losses. To compensate members for losses from predators, self-insurance schemes are developing. These schemes currently have backing from NGOs and some outside funding. They also cover losses resulting from damage by wild animals to people, crops and property. And, as conservancies earn income from tourist activities, some choose to use their income to dig waterholes for elephants to keep them away from homesteads.

As the example of community-based natural resource management in Namibia shows us, in some situations creating new property rights by legislation will effectively expand a bundle of rights. Key issues to consider are: Does the property legislation work in a positive, symbiotic manner with other legal requirements? Is the legislation an exercise in rent-seeking whereby a few benefit at the expense of many? Does the legislation reflect social norms about the appropriate uses of property? Certainly, it seems that one criterion for effectively creating property rights is the existence of a relatively stable surrounding institutional environment that includes a meaningful rule of law and a regulatory regime that facilitates business activity. For the most part, this exists in Namibia.

Property titling in South Africa

Another example of taking the legislative path to property is the South African government's programme to transfer legal title over residential property to residents of townships. The movement in several countries in the developing world to provide legal titles for informal property received a strong boost from Hernando de Soto's writing, which strongly argues for formalisation (De Soto, 2000). Titling efforts are not new in Africa, however: Kenya's colonial-era titling programme is perhaps the best-known example of a government-driven effort to create more individualised rights to land in sub-Saharan Africa (Ensminger, 1997: 175–91; Pinckney and Kimuyu, 1994; Coldham, 1979: 615–27).[2]

In the case of South Africa, the ANC government's efforts to transfer title from municipalities, which rented housing to black South Africans under the apartheid system, to residents were an important part of the transition towards a more democratic country and also addressed serious housing concerns (Boudreaux, 2006).[3] To take one case, in the 1990s the city of Cape Town began transferring titles to residents of Langa township. Langa is an old township to the south-east of Cape Town that was created after World War I. Previous governments had built a combination of dormitory/hostel housing for male workers and some concrete-block houses for families. Title to these concrete-block houses has now shifted from the municipal government to the local residents. Given the current institutional environment in South Africa, these titles seem to be secure.

The benefits of this change in legal rights track fairly closely with other such efforts in the developing world: new owners have incentives to improve their property because they will now directly

---

2   The long experience of the Kenyan government with titling efforts is both fascinating and instructive. For a discussion of the titling process with a focus on why land is reverting to customary-law rules and ignoring formal titling provisions, see Ensminger (1997) and Coldham (1979).

3   See Boudreaux (2006). In 1978 the National Party government introduced the 99-year lease for black South Africans. Six years later, the government passed the Communities Development Act that created a statutory right to register these leases, beginning in 1986. This Act allowed residents to begin the process of converting leasehold tenure into freehold tenure. This allowed the government to begin privatising the housing stock for black South Africans. A host of problems limited the effectiveness of this process. Actual transfer of titles did not take place until after the election of the ANC Unity government in 1994.

benefit from such efforts. Many of the homeowners in Langa have installed new windows, expanded their homes, upgraded kitchens and other parts of the interior. These upgrades help to support a local artisan class of masons, carpenters, bricklayers and painters. Home supply and hardware stores have more customers from the townships. Adebayo and Adebayo report: 'The housing process can have important links with the informal sector. The informal construction industry, constituting very small firms and private individuals can itself be a major source of employment much needed by the urban poor' (2000: 5). Owners, in turn, have an even more valuable asset.

Few homeowners, however, use their titles as collateral for commercial loans. Home improvements are paid for from personal savings or from the proceeds of a savings club. People open businesses in their homes but few rely on home loans to fund these ventures. Instead, home improvements are made incrementally and, once complete, owners have an asset that is debt-free.

There is a township property market in South Africa and this market has strengthened recently. In Langa, people do sell their homes, but many of the sales are informal and the buyer and seller use signed affidavits rather than more formal sales contracts. When these informal sales take place, titles are not registered in the Registrar's Office, so the registry quickly loses relevance.

What explains the real-estate situation in Langa? People do respond to realignments in incentives when they receive a secure title. They expend time and energy on improving their home. Many factors combine, however, to make the use of commercial credit quite low. First, the unemployment rate in South Africa is high, upwards of 26 per cent. Many people therefore work in the informal sector and do not have payslips they can show to mortgage bond officers who issue bank loans. Informal sector workers are also perceived as riskier borrowers. Moreover, many homeowners have extended family members and/or renters living with them as a result of the severe housing shortage in the country. If a homeowner took a mortgage loan and defaulted, he or she would risk losing housing for many people and might risk losing supplemental rental income. In addition, many people create informal businesses, such as spaza shops or shebeens, in their homes. If title is used as collateral and a borrower defaults, this puts a family business at risk as well.

Further, there is little lending directed at low-income borrowers – few banking offices are located in townships (this may be changing, though) and few loans are made to those earning less than R5,000 per month (approximately $710). High interest rates and banking fees combine to make it expensive for borrowers to use banks. Moreover, banks have had a poor experience in terms of repossessing property in townships, and there are few alternatives to traditional mortgage lending in Africa (McAuslan, 2006). This raises the cost of doing business in these areas. Thus, this has not been a profitable market for banks and few operate in townships, though again, this does seem to be changing. In addition, restrictive labour laws and the ill effects of the apartheid era combine to create an institutional environment that is not conducive to the widespread use of titles as collateral among low-income earners.

Transfers take place informally for several reasons. In South Africa only specialist conveyancing attorneys may legally transfer title to property. These monopolistic providers are able to charge high fees for their services and these costs may be excessively burdensome for some sellers. In addition, titles may be transferred only if sellers can prove that they have paid all local taxes that are owed to the municipality and all service fees. Many residents are years behind in these payments and do not, or cannot, pay the amounts owing to transfer their title legally. Formal transfer is, therefore, too costly for many, so they opt to transfer homes informally, a process some have referred to as an 'informal formalization' (Lund et al., 2006: 21).

Given these various difficulties, one might ask if the capital in Langa is dead or alive. Titles are secure and formal, and there is a property market, but the general institutional environment is fraught with informality. As a result, capital is more sluggish than it might be. The government's policy of transferring title was certainly beneficial to residents, who now hold a more valuable asset. By giving residents additional sticks in the bundle of property rights, the government has created incentives for owners to invest in, maintain and improve property. This incentive translates into support for local artisans and provides employment in a country that suffers from high unemployment rates. For this market to provide further benefits, however, the high transaction costs that spur informal transfer must be reduced. Labour laws need to be revised to make it easier to employ people and build businesses. Banks need to be confident that mortgage contracts will be upheld.

The South African government's policy of transferring title from the public sector to private individuals has been an important step on the road towards formalisation and improved economic development (De Soto, 2000). The policy has, however, carried South Africa only part of the way towards poverty alleviation. On-the-ground realities and institutional complexities make it difficult for Langa's residents to use their titles as collateral. The experience in Langa illustrates both the embeddedness of institutions and the complexities associated with property-rights creation and reform. While some proponents have offered titling as the path to prosperity for the developing world, experience counsels caution. Titling is not a panacea and cannot, by itself, miraculously whisk the poor from the world of informality into the commercial world.

> ### Box 2 Property rights in China
> Over the past two decades, mainland China has experienced sustained economic growth rates of between 7 and 9 per cent per annum. Market reforms sparked this tremendous growth, which has led to a massive shift of population from rural areas and agricultural work to urban areas and jobs in the manufacturing sector. Although the government limits political freedom, it has created and sustained an environment in which businesses, both domestic and foreign, feel confident operating.
>
> China seems to be something of an institutional outlier. If strong institutions are essential for economic development, how can one explain the success of this communist country? After all, China has a weak property-rights environment and a weak judicial system, yet the country attracts significant flows of foreign direct investment. Why do investors feel secure in a country that, until 2006, did not allow individuals to own land (though it did allow long-term leases)?
>
> As Zhang (2005) argues, the answer may lie in the national government's fiscal decentralisation efforts. Quicksilver capital moves with relative ease from one jurisdiction to another, seeking a combination of high returns and security. Local governments in China compete to attract investors who bring revenue to the jurisdiction. This revenue is used to provide

public goods and services. Importantly, Zhang notes that local officials receive promotions and other benefits based upon how much investment they attract. The result is that local government officials, who are often in partnership with businesses operating town village enterprises (TVEs), work hard to provide stable and secure environments for doing business. Discussing these enterprises, Zhang (ibid.: 2) says:

> Although the TVEs did not have clearly defined property rights, the sector has achieved remarkable growth. To explain this puzzle, Li (1996) developed a model of how ambiguous property rights can lead to growth. Due to the lack of formal protections on property rights, the uncertainty related to doing business is very high. As a result, the transaction cost to write a complete contract is often prohibitive. In this context, the ambiguous property rights arrangement, which often involved local officials as shareholders of TVEs, may be a better option because it can help secure protection from the local government and reduce impediments to reform at the local level.

Ambiguous property rights, at least ambiguous de jure rights, are efficient in such a scenario: they allow for local-level property-rights entrepreneurship by government officials. While national-level property-rights protections may be weak, local-level protections are fairly strong. In this case, a gap exists between the de jure rules (which are weak) and the de facto norms (which are strong).

Strong protection for the rights of investors has a negative flip side, however: individual property rights in China, particularly the rights of rural people to secure land, are weak.

Local government officials may do a good job of protecting the rights of investors, but they too often do this at the expense of local farmers and other local residents, who are forced to sell rights to land, allegedly for 'public' purposes, and are forcibly removed from land in order to provide space for new commercial entities. Local governments decide what compensation farmers should receive for their land. By one estimate (ibid.: 15) farmers typically receive 5–10 per cent of total market value. Not surprisingly, the incidence of land-related conflict and protest in China has soared. What the results of this social conflict will be are unclear, but as Zhang argues '[i]n the short run, the weak protection of individual property rights may fuel economic growth because it reduced the transaction costs of acquiring land … [b]ut in the long run, it may have profound and negative economic and social consequences' (ibid.: 17). By creating relatively thick bundles of property rights for one class of people – investors – local Chinese governments have provided an institutional environment conducive to economic growth. Decentralisation and jurisdictional competition have benefited some at the expense of many. Perhaps China is not so much of an outlier after all.

Box 3 Property rights in Russia

Russia, like China, has experienced massive change over the past two decades. The transition from a communist past to an authoritarian present has, for many, been painful. The country lost ground economically while privatisation efforts were viewed as a failure.

The comparison with the Chinese case provides a useful contrast. There is evidence that local governments in China have, over the past two decades, created de facto property rights for investors which, in turn, led to economic growth. The property-rights environment in Russia presents a different scenario. In his 1998 article, Michael Heller painted a picture of a transition country with extremely fragmented property rights. He argued that the post-Soviet government adopted a privatisation strategy that gave too many individuals undesirably thin bundles of rights to some classes of property, particularly commercial and industrial properties: '[t]ransition regimes have often failed to endow any individual with a bundle of rights that represents full ownership of storefronts or other scarce resources' (Heller, 1998: 623).

Although the government gave 'powerful socialist-era stakeholders' transferable sticks in property-rights bundles, other individuals held some rights to the same property. The result was a tragedy of the anti-commons: 'multiple owners are each endowed with the right to exclude others from a scarce resource, and no-one has an effective privilege of use' (ibid.: 624). Heller argues that individuals had difficulty overcoming the tragedy because of high transaction costs, strategic behaviour and biases that made informal negotiating to exercise ownership rights ineffective. The result was underutilised resources and limited economic growth.

In a situation with excessively fragmented rights, owners can attempt to rebundle rights through market forces or through government action. Heller argues that 'existing rights-holders, including local government agencies and the private actors who have invested in reliance on the current property regime, may cling tenaciously to their rights'. Rent-seeking behaviour by existing rights-holders may result in government inaction. Negotiations to rebundle rights may therefore have to take place 'through informal or corrupt channels. Over time, these corrupt channels can be routinized and may replace legal transactions' (ibid.: 641).

Sonin (2002) argues that in Russia wealthy individuals, those who have successfully rebundled rights and who rely on private property-rights enforcement, may prefer weak to strong public protection of property rights:

> Economic agents are forced to supplement their productive investment with investment in private protection. With economies of scale in private protection, rich agents have a significant advantage when operating in an environment with incomplete public protection of property rights. Furthermore, their ability to gain from redistribution due to improper protection of property rights makes them natural opponents of improvements in public protection. (ibid.: 2)

Privatisation in Russia may have failed, at least in part, because property rights to newly privatised resources were excessively fragmented. Because the public sector was not able to effectively rebundle rights, individuals used alternative means to create thicker bundles and used private methods to enforce rights to these bundles. Those entrepreneurs who successfully created thick bundles of rights and protected these rights privately had disincentives to support effective property-rights reform. The resulting 'subversion of institutions' (Glaeser et al., 2003) may help explain Russia's difficult transition to a market economy.

6 THE EVOLUTIONARY PATH

If institutions are evolving, dynamic arrangements, how can we best take into account the various 'moving pieces' within the structure? Customary law is evolved law, having changed over time to meet specific needs in specific environments. In many cases, particularly in Africa, customary law may provide a greater degree of tenure security than formal law. This raises the question: is the better path for securing property rights in Africa to somehow formalise customary rights and privileges (Alden Wiley, 2006)? There are no simple answers here either, as this approach is also fraught with complexity and uncertainty and not free from problems associated with rent-seeking behaviours (Durand-Lasserve, 2006).

While it is clear that communities often respond to increasing demands for property by moving towards greater individualisation of property rights, we should not, however, expect such movements to be free of controversy. When societies shift from communal to individualised rights, those persons who previously had responsibility for allocating rights are likely to lose power and status within their community. Some individuals, particularly those with greater clout in the society, are likely to receive rights to more valuable parcels, or to larger parcels, than more marginalised members of the society. These changes may engender conflict, but unless the society develops an effective alternative method for meeting the increased demand for land (via effective land markets, for example) it may experience even greater levels of conflict.

The evolution of property rights in Plateau, Nigeria

One example of how property rights evolve and how blocking that process by legislation can lead to conflict comes from Nigeria. The central part of the country is dominated by a plateau – a highland that was lightly populated until the twentieth century. In the nineteenth century this rugged area was home to a heterogeneous population composed of small ethnic groups living independently from their neighbour to the north, the Muslim Sultanate of Sokoto, and their neighbours to the south, Igos, Ijaws and Edos, among others.

Britain took control of Nigeria in 1900 and created Northern and Southern Nigeria. The British also created different formal property environments in these two regions. In the south, property could be owned individually. Land registries existed to facilitate individual sale. In the north, land was essentially nationalised, with the government granting long-term permits to occupy. In the Plateau region, it seems that customary law probably lasted longer than in the other regions with local chiefs acting as native authorities and acting through native courts, making use and allocation decisions over land (Falola, 1999: 70–72).

The ethnic groups in Plateau had an abundance of different customary land-law rules. Property rules included norms for excluding outsiders, for incorporating outsiders via adoption, for lending/borrowing land, for inheriting land and for pledging property in satisfaction of a debt. Other rules governed physical structures erected on land and valuable trees.[1] People living in Plateau had many sticks in a bundle of property rights and these sticks provided flexibility and opportunity to community members. Although community members typically did not hold the stick that allowed for the sale or transfer of property, the norm of pledging land could approximate a sale so long as the pledge went unredeemed.

Reports from British officials in Nigeria in the 1930s testify that, in the eastern part of Plateau, people who cultivated land held it under rules that resembled freehold property (Boudreaux, 2005b: 61–102).[2] Their property could be sold, but not leased or pawned. In the northern part of Plateau, in the Jos region, land could be leased for long periods but land sales were rare, except around Ganawuri, a town with fertile land. In the southern part of Plateau the Kofyar people adopted intensive permanent cultivation techniques and expended tremendous effort creating terraces on hillsides. These terraces were a costly investment and, not surprisingly, people who made these investments had highly individualised rights to the land. Writing in the 1960s about these hill farmers, anthropologist Robert Netting says:

> The Kofyar insist that every square inch of arable soil, both village and bush, has an owner, a single person to whom the land belongs and who alone may decide on its use. This is probably a direct outgrowth of intensive farming. Wherever land can be made to produce heavily and continuously over a long period of time, it increased in value to both the occupant and his heirs. (Netting, 1968: 159)

---

1 For a discussion of customary land law in Africa, see Olawale Elias (1962).
2 See Boudreaux (2005b) for an extended discussion of the relationship between insecure property rights and violence in Plateau State.

Interestingly, the Kofyar moved away from intensive cultivation in the 1950s, towards cash cropping and then, in the 1970s, back to permanent settlements with a renewed effort at intensive cultivation (Netting et al., 1989: 299–319). The key point is that customary land-law rules were flexible enough in Plateau to allow for the increasing individualisation of property rights in response to the increasing value of land. Indeed, property in Plateau existed on a continuum from traditional communal rights towards something closely approximating freehold.

Residents of Plateau were travelling on an evolutionary path to property that was blocked by the Land Use Act, which nationalised land in Nigeria. This 1978 legislation shifted land allocation decisions to state governors, who are empowered to issue certificates of occupancy. Although the statute was supposed to 'rationalise' the complex system of customary, statutory and common-law rules governing land in Nigeria, as well as curb land speculation, the law provides many opportunities for side payments and corruption as certificate-holders must seek approval from state governors to gift their certificates, sell them or otherwise use them (not to mention obtaining them in the first place). Combine problems of corruption with liberal use of compulsory acquisition by the government and the Land Use Act creates an insecure property-rights environment in which individuals have bundles of property rights that are relatively thin.

This centralised and politicised process for land allocation removed the power to allocate land from traditional authorities. Donald Williams argues that the Nigerian land law 'was designed to pose a direct challenge to alternative sources of societal authority by relegating all private transactions in land to government agencies' (Williams, 1992: 587). The legislative process for allocating land in Nigeria, which is open to corruption, may also exacerbate conflict between groups, such as farmers and pastoralists, who in the past managed to share land but who now compete for land as Nigeria's population rises and as desertification sends more people from northern Nigeria into the central part of the country.

We would expect that in a situation where the demand for land increases as population rises, and as heterogeneity (hence transaction costs) increases as well, communities would expend additional resources defining property rights more clearly and defending those rights against others. In Nigeria, this redefinition cannot take place because of the nationalisation of land (or it does not take place in any formal sense, it takes place de facto). Because it is so costly to establish property rights under the Land Use Act, people may turn to informal, extra-legal means to protect land when outsiders encroach on it. The Act creates a situation of tenure insecurity and in this situation people may choose personal justice – fighting – and de facto rights over the current system. In Plateau, as in other parts of Africa that suffer from resource conflict, thousands of people have lost their lives in battles over property.[3] This is one of the most important aspects of secure property rights: they reduce conflict by clarifying rights and by providing the means to enforce rights through peaceful means.

---

3   'Nigeria: Plateau state violence claimed 53,000 lives – report', *UN Integrated Regional Information Networks*, 8 October 2004, *www.irennews.org/reprt. asp?ReportID=43580*.

Land ownership and cocoa production in western Ghana

Ghana provides a different example of the evolutionary path to property in Africa. Land devoted to cocoa production is controlled by rules of customary law. The right to use it for agricultural purposes was traditionally given to family groups by local leaders. As the area available for planting cocoa trees has dwindled, owing to an influx of migrants and rising local population, land rules have evolved from a system of communal rights towards more individualised property rights. Quisumbing et al. write that:

> [In western Ghana] [u]ncultivated forestland is owned by the community or village, and the village chief serves as the custodian of forest area. In reality, village forest is open access for the community members, as was the case also for migrants when the forestland was abundant. Thus, the clearance of forest is easily approved by the chief, so long as forestland is available. Forest clearance requires a large effort, and those who clear forests are rewarded by relatively strong individual rights to land. Such individually rewarded land rights are further strengthened if land converters make long-term or permanent improvements in the land such as tree planting. (Quisumbing et al., 2001: 55)[4]

The authors go on to note that property rights weaken when land lies fallow for extended periods of time. Over time, rules

---

4 See Quisumbing et al. (2001: 55). The authors note (p. 56) that these changes may have been strengthened by the passage, in 1985, of the Intestate Succession Law, which allows wives and children to inherit land from husbands who die intestate, something that was not possible under older customary law. This may be a case of legislation reflecting changing social norms, though the opposite could also be true: the law may have pushed social norms towards greater individualisation of property rights.

regarding the transfer of land have also changed. In the past, when land was plentiful, property devolved to nephews and other male family members. But as property has become increasingly scarce, and valuable, more men are giving property directly to their wives and children with the consent of family members. These gifts of property occur during the man's life and are formalised in ceremonies. Once the gift is given, the new owners have individualised rights to the land.

Migrants to cocoa-producing areas have also developed more individualised rights to property over time. In their case, some property is acquired through gifts, but more is acquired through sales and rental arrangements. The latter call for migrants to clear forestland, plant it with cocoa trees and tend the trees for a period of time, after which the ownership of the land will be divided between the original owner and the migrant (ibid.: 62). '[L]and scarcity stimulates land market transactions,' Quisumbing et al. argue (ibid.: 55). And land markets will allow some individuals to consolidate holdings, a prospect that some will find undesirable but others will see as paving the way for productivity gains in cocoa production, with benefits for cocoa farmers, their families and, the authors argue, the local environment. In western Ghana and other areas, people will often plant trees in order to establish stronger individualised land rights. Land that people wish to transfer through a gift is most often planted with cocoa trees as a way of creating stronger rights for a relatively new class of property claimants: wives and children. As the authors note: 'It is a mistake to assume that incentives to invest in land governed by customary land tenure rules are universally very weak' (ibid.: 64). With a detailed understanding of the local property-rights environment, these authors were able to describe its evolutionary nature.

Individualisation and formalisation

Will communal property inevitably transform into individualised, freehold property? Probably not; in some situations it remains the case that the costs associated with this move are prohibitive. Communal property serves particular needs for some societies (social insurance and risk-sharing, among others). In addition: 'property conventions, norms, and customs are often more predictable and unchanging than statutory law itself' (Blocher, 2006: 173). There is no reason to expect an inexorable move from communal to individual property under customary systems. The shift should happen in response to changing conditions and changes in the relative value of resources. As a given community experiments with new ways to adapt, it may opt for more individualised property rights or it may not.

A related question is whether changes towards greater individualisation inevitably lead to the creation of legal titles to property. Platteau argues they may not, and for good reason: so long as rights to use and 'gift' or rent the land are secure and defendable, formal titles might be desirable but not necessary for economic development (Platteau, 1996: 27–86). Alternatives to formal land titling exist. For example in Uganda the government registers certificates of customary ownership. This less formal process of securing tenure is facilitated by technological advances. Countries may use a geographical information database/system (GIS) that captures details about land parcels, rather than a more elaborate cadastral system (Sanjak, 2004). Sanjak notes: 'These systems [GIS] have the potential to make information more reliable and easier to obtain, thus making it easier to understand and price risk. This is especially important where court systems are neither efficient nor equitable and where access to and quality of information on real property has been problematic.' Formal titling programmes and cadastral registries are costly to create and implement effectively, so their creation and management will involve difficult trade-offs for developing nations – trade-offs between the potential for increased legal certainty over the status of ownership and other desirable social goals.

Do these examples offer any lessons about the evolutionary path to property? The evolutionary path is not perfect – it can be usurped and used to benefit some groups or individuals over others. The process of rule change under customary law can be slow and frustrating, but the system does promote flexibility. Given that customary law is an organic system, it may reflect the customs and social norms of the group to which it applies more closely than legislation. If so, there would be less reason to be concerned about a gap between de facto property rights and *de jure* property rights. Reducing gaps between the two may help lessen conflict. Further, in societies with predatory centralised governments, an evolutionary path that relies on customary law to allocate and enforce property rights may provide an important counterbalance to political power.

7 SUMMING UP: FIAT AND EVOLUTION

These limited examples do not by any means capture the full richness of Africa's property environment and its evolution. There are many other case studies and problems related to property that could be discussed. These few examples are intended to give concrete empirical substance to our abstract discussion of the complexity of property-rights systems (and the strategies of changing these systems) by highlighting some of the issues and concerns related to creating secure property rights in the developing-world context. These cases illustrate, in tangible terms, the benefits and limits of real-world efforts to create property rights along the continuum of possible approaches.

By looking at how property has evolved in various situations we can better appreciate the intricate trajectories of change. For instance, we have seen how customary law provided for relatively thick bundles of rights in a communal setting. So long as land (or another resource) remains abundant, communal systems do a good job of allocating rights to use and otherwise benefit from the resource. In a situation of resource abundance, these communal or customary rights tend to be secure vis-à-vis the rest of the communal group. These rights become less secure, however, when they need to be enforced on outsiders (who follow different norms). Transaction costs rise as locals must bargain and contract with strangers. Unless the groups have strong trading ties with each other, trust levels are likely to be low. Customary-law systems seem to have a difficult time overcoming these high transaction costs and offering security to people within and outside the original communal group. These difficulties often lead to conflict, which, in turn, can spur government intervention – with mixed results. In other cases governments neglect these conflicts – and unresolved conflicts can contribute to more serious problems.

Rights also become less secure when internal population pressure or new opportunities to use land raise its value. As the value of land rises individuals have incentives to capture more of that value by creating more individualised rights. Group members may be willing to violate existing social norms in order to capture this value, leading to internal conflict, as was the case with the Samburu. Alternatively, individuals who are especially well connected in the group's social network may signal that a shift towards more individualised rights will ultimately benefit everyone. In this way, these connected individuals help push social norms in the direction of individualisation. This seems to be the case, for example, with the Galole Orma people in Kenya. Indeed, one of the virtues of customary law is that it allows evolutionary transition from communal rights to more individualised rights, such as happened in Nigeria in the Plateau area before 1978.

The evolutionary path of the customary law is not perfect. The transition process from communal to individualised property rights is often conflict-ridden. The process may result in elites, or subsets of the community, seeking (and acquiring) more favourable property dispositions than others. It may lead to farmers battling herders over rights to fertile land or water sources. It may also be the case that the evolutionary path does not move quickly enough for some critics. For example, social norms may prevent women from acquiring secure property rights upon the death of their husbands. The evolutionary system does, however, reflect local experimentation designed to meet local needs.

In short, both theory and empirical evidence show that there is no single formula to help customary systems' transition from secure communal rights to secure individualised rights in a peaceful manner. Sometimes this transition happens spontaneously, but this is not necessarily the case. So long as the move towards more individualised rights places few restrictions on the sale of property, we would, over time, expect to see the gains from the creation of new property rights spread more broadly. Because the evolutionary path creates property rights in a decentralised fashion, there should be fewer opportunities for rent-seeking than exist when property rights are created by a centralised authority.

The evolutionary path may also be more conducive to experimentation with different property rules than a centralised, legislative approach. Much legislation adopts a one-size-fits-all solution that is less flexible and adaptable, and therefore less likely to meet divergent social needs, than an evolutionary approach. In some cases, however, the legislative route can be a more reliable way to create secure property rights. This path to property may work most effectively when it devolves property rights to individuals, broadening the property franchise rather than constricting it. In the case of community-based natural resource management in Namibia and property titling in Langa township, South Africa, we see examples of governments devolving sticks in the bundle of property rights to citizens. This devolution increases opportunities for the new rights-holders to trade their property, to use it creatively to further their personal goals and to protect themselves against the predatory behaviour of others. Property is secure when predation is limited.

It remains the case in Africa that secure communal rights will be appropriate in some situations. In cases where a resource is becoming increasingly scarce, however, secure individualised rights are both feasible and desirable. The question of how best to move from communal rights to individualised rights is not settled and could not be settled in abstract terms. Sometimes this transition happens spontaneously through the customary law. In other cases, new rights can be created legislatively. There is no one way to accomplish this desirable goal – no 'one-size-fits-all' solution to the problem of insecure property rights in the developing world. In the light of this overview we can better appreciate the complexity of the range of possible approaches between the two ideal types, evolutionary and by fiat. Yet operational questions remain. How do we assess such complex evolutionary processes and our capacities to steer them in directions that are good for economic development and growth? How do we decide when it is necessary to have a top-down, legislative, formal intervention? How should those interventions be calibrated to fit the institutional and social context?

8 AN INTELLECTUAL TOOLBOX FOR THE CREATION OF PROPERTY RIGHTS

The international development community – policy analysts, economists, decision-makers, donors – quite often sees its role as 'fixing' economies and setting them on the path of growth, much as doctors cure patients, or engineers repair very complex machines. Whether we fully accept this analogy or not, it clearly implies that in order to fulfil such a task both theoretical and practical knowledge are needed. Those involved in designing development strategies should understand the specifics of the cases they address and also understand the conditions and instruments of institutional change.

In dealing with property-rights creation, as in many other cases of institutional change, the main challenge is to find a balance between general knowledge and local knowledge, between change via evolution with its (often) gradual shifts in informal rules and norms and change via legislation with its shifts in formal rules. As noted above, the available strategies are defined by the various combinations of the two extremes: the spontaneous, bottom-up, evolutionary route and the top-down, precisely targeted, fiat approach, taking into account the many factors that will impact the implementation and enforcement of rights. The real-life practice in policy and institutional design strategy requires us to position our approaches on this spectrum of possible positions, as there is no unique solution. Finding a balance between the two extreme types requires fine tuning and calibration on a case-by-case basis.

This does not mean, however, that we are left with arbitrary alternatives. There are ways to obtain discipline and focus. One can better marry design to reality when informed by a specific conceptual framework rooted in the accumulated experience of property-rights policies in international development. In other words, property-rights policies could deal with complexity and the difficult task of finding an appropriate balance between different approaches by making reference to a set of insights derived from the accumulated findings of scholarly research and practical experience. One could think of these both as lessons based on past experiences and as intellectual tools in the toolbox of the designer of property-rights systems.

The process view of property-rights systems

Some international development agencies have begun to recognise that all institutions, including property rights, are part and parcel of a dynamic system (USAID, 2007). The factors that determine the property-rights configurations are many, complex and volatile, and changes in these factors will have unmistakable consequences. Property rights transform, adapt and reconfigure. For example, changes in property-rights technology can alter the costs associated with defining, enforcing or transferring rights. In turn, changes in these costs may alter the structure of the property-rights arrangement. In similar ways, informal rules may be altered in response to increasing scarcity or owing to changes in the values and beliefs shaping them. One may also expect property rights to be affected by developments in knowledge and technology. The transition from public to private property or the move from common to more individualised property should not be seen as an isolated sequence of events but rather as elements of a larger process. The movement from public to private (whether individual or common property) simultaneously creates and destroys rights, and this creation and destruction will have distributional effects.

Even when a property-rights configuration has stabilised within the private-property category, there are still various arrangements and forms in that category that get continually shaped and reshaped by contextual factors. This is in no way a mechanical process: in many cases the various configurations of property rights are a matter of sequencing and path dependency. If public or regulatory property emerges first, then the incentives for the discovery of private-property-rights technology may be weakened (Yandle, 2001). The process moves on specific paths and not on others. If the above is correct, then it is a mistake to limit our view of property rights to a mere static configuration of rules and laws and an associated set of incentives. To sum up: a process view of property rights puts their nature in better perspective and is entirely justifiable.

Property rights are in fact elements of an ongoing social process proceeding as the technological, social and economic environment is changing – a fact that many advocates of property rights (in all their forms) tend to forget. They assume a static view, which assumes that arrangements are frozen in place or aims at creating such arrangements. But this may be both theoretically and practically misleading. The fundamental objective of the property-rights initiatives may get distorted. Seen through the process lens, the policy objective is not just to create a specific configuration but to create an institutional structure able to respond dynamically to ongoing changes in costs, technologies, social circumstances, etc. In other words, the objective would be the fluidity of the property-rights bundles so that they were free to adjust as changes in costs thresholds or changes in public or individual preferences became evident.

These observations correspond with a more general point of social theory and institutional policy made by Norman Barry. As Barry puts it, there are two basic traditions competing in social and political theory: an 'end-state' (or final outcome) approach and a 'process' (a chain of causes and consequences) approach. The end-state social theory attempts an understanding of social phenomena through 'a description of the features of a society at a specified point in time' – especially the features predetermining the society's distribution of income, wealth, power, prestige, status and the structures of the economic and political systems. On the normative side, it creates an ideal, a final state or goal, and declares its implementation the final purpose of politics (Barry, 1998: 25). In contrast, there is the process theory, which supports a 'decentralised activity, interaction and co-ordination of social action and shuns away from the government direction or planning designed to produce a predetermined state' (ibid.):

> They may also be called procedural theories, since they are pre-eminently concerned with the nature of the rules in an orderly, regularized society; acting and choosing individuals who follow them can be said to generate certain end-states. Social scientists who analyse processes that produce end-states are especially interested in constitutions. Their evaluation will thus not be confined to the end-state itself but will focus essentially on the procedural rules and human actions that generated it. (ibid.: 26)

Seen from this perspective, one of the common fallacies in the strategies of creating or reforming property rights is to think exclusively in terms of end-states and neglect thinking in terms of process. As we have seen, when dealing with property rights we are dealing with complex dynamics involving a multitude of factors. A change of emphasis from end-states to process has important practical implications. Rather than being fixated with a particular, unchangeable configuration of rights, the change process itself becomes just as important as the favoured arrangement. Instead of unfreezing an institutional arrangement just to refreeze it in a new configuration, the goal becomes making the system flexible, adaptable and resilient, resonating closely with the preferences of individuals on the ground. Such an approach implies special attention to exchange, transfer and transactions factors, and to the communication and exchange of information needed for coordination among rights-holders or stakeholders (Yandle, 2001: 8). Transfers and transactions based on the voluntary decisions of the holders and stakeholders are the ways through which the readjustment intrinsic to a dynamic and responsive property-rights system takes place. The process view can therefore be operationalised by creating the institutional conditions to facilitate such exchanges.

Adopting the idea of process implies the acceptance of the irreducible tension between the process view and the end-state view and with it the paradox of process thinking. Whether we like it or not, even when advocating a process view, we explicitly or implicitly operate with an end-state in mind: the end-state is merely shifted at a meta level. It simply becomes the 'constitutional' framework that facilitates the property-rights process, a framework that defines the parameters of the optimal dynamics of the process. This observation draws on the work of Elinor Ostrom, who introduces the distinction between the operational level, the collective-choice level and the constitutional level as a useful way of understanding the complexity of human action within institutional frameworks (Ostrom, 2005). *Constitutional-level* rules determine how a group may craft collective-choice rules that in turn govern the way future collective decisions are made. The *collective-choice level* is the level at which 'officials' determine, enforce or alter the basic framework within which actions take place. Legislation is a well-documented example of collective-choice rules (Hayek, 1973). Finally, the *operational level* is the level of everyday life decisions.

Under this schematic, the meta level (constitutive level) is the framework within which the rules governing future collective decisions are determined. The bottom or operational level consists of direct actions and rules depending on and directly reacting to everyday, concrete circumstances and expectations. The sphere of action and scope of decision-making at this level are established by the other, higher levels. These operational actions and decisions, however, affect the higher levels in an indirect and aggregate way. In the end, a feedback loop is always possible, leading to the gradual alteration of the meta level.

The daily activity in a market nicely illustrates such decisions. Public choice and constitutional rules are gradually changed as a result of the dynamics set into motion by the exchange process. If market relations *do* promote changes not only in the allocation and production of resources but also in norms and institutions, towards higher levels of social efficiency, fairness and trust, then expanding opportunities for trade may positively affect the different layers by making the property systems of a society more functional and secure.

The interplay of the formal and informal

For those interested in property-rights reform it is essential to understand whether or not the de facto property environment matches or tracks de jure rules. This is a recurring theme in both the institutionalist and land-tenure literature. Authors such as Ensminger point to 'the importance of *complementarities* between informal and formal institutions' (Ensminger, 1997: 166). She argues that: '[w]hen formal systems are imposed upon a society with which they are out of accord, self-enforcement may erode and externally engineered incentives may fail to yield the predicted results' (ibid.).

If, for example, the de facto environment, and the social norms that support it, are opposed to particular property allocations (such as women inheriting property or property rights shifting towards individualisation), the de jure creation of such allocations may be a fruitless exercise. If the institutional environment is weak and de jure property rights cannot be exercised (because it is too costly to do so), a gap exists and property reformers would be well advised to attend to the institutional weaknesses if they hope to create meaningful benefits for the de jure rights-holders.

Understanding the de facto property environment will help reformers understand who may gain and who may lose if rules change. With this knowledge, reformers will be better equipped to identify or create coalitions to support any legislative changes in favour of individualisation (if that path is desirable). And finally, with an understanding of the de facto situation, reformers will be better able to identify possible property-rights entrepreneurs or those who can push positive changes in norms.

It is relatively easy to initiate changes to a nation's legal code. Creating an environment in which property rights are both broadened (provided to more citizens) and made more secure, however, will take more than an addition to the appropriate section of the constitution, land law or other property statute. Creating such a secure property-rights environment will require policymakers to adopt an integrated approach that identifies related deficiencies in the judicial and police systems, reduces transaction costs for registering property claims, recognises and understands how social norms relate to the proposed change and works with the various stakeholders affected – those who stand to lose from the changes as well as those who stand to gain. Without this deep local knowledge of the de facto property rights and their environment, top-down legislative approaches are unlikely to succeed.

Incentives, costs and the critical role of economic thresholds

Those promoting reforms should keep in mind the important fact that property rights have an economic basis. In other words, there are economic thresholds beyond which it is cost-effective or economically rational to introduce property rights (Kagwanja, 2006). Conversely there are thresholds under which costs hinder their emergence. In some situations people have incentives to define, create and enforce property rights, while under different circumstances such incentives are lacking. It has already been pointed out that the standard narrative of the emergence of property rights begins with a situation illustrated by the 'tragedy of the commons' and ends with some proposed property-rights solution. This is a story of economic thresholds. The initial property arrangement may vary: common, public or private property rights. But in all cases, an investment in a costly mechanism to define, monitor and enforce the right is required. Irrespective of its specific form, a right requires instruments and costs to keep it in existence. Thus economic considerations are introduced into the picture. The threshold beyond which it becomes economically feasible to sustain the property rights in question is an indirect measure of the availability of those instruments. Only when it is cost-effective to claim, define, monitor and/or enforce a certain right is it possible for a property-rights arrangement to emerge (Demsetz, 1967; Anderson and Hill, 1975, 2001; Barzel, 1997; Libecap, 1989; Ostrom, 1990).

The notion of 'economic threshold' could be further elaborated as it usually implies the existence of several conditions (Yandle, 2001: 1–2). The demand dimension of the threshold is one of these. This threshold is reached when the resources at issue increase in value owing to growing demand. Increasing demand for a resource changes the opportunity costs of investing in the instruments needed to maintain the rights over it. But this is just one aspect of the problem. For the property-rights threshold to be met, cost-effective technologies for measuring, monitoring and enclosing must also exist. Without appropriate technologies the task of identifying units of the resource, so that they may be claimed and transferred, may be impossible. Even at a constant demand for resources, the declining cost of the technologies could lead to a breaking point. Once these technologies become available, the conditions for property rights to emerge are in place. This was the case in the American West with the invention of barbed wire, a low-cost technology available to enclose, and hence readily identify, property rights (see below).

An additional economic dimension is given by the problem

of wealth-distribution effects. People may accept or reject a property-rights arrangement based on how they perceive its distributional consequences. Only when the impact of the redistribution is mitigated in acceptable forms is it likely that a property-rights arrangement will be relatively stable (Libecap, 1989: 11–12). One may have a situation in which demand for property rights and the technology to define and enforce them exist, but the arrangement is unsustainable because of distributive issues. Side payments may be required to satisfy those interested in maintaining the status quo. The exact forms the property rights take are affected by this factor. If the distributional cost hurdle is too high, individualised property rights may not emerge. Political or regulatory property rights will emerge instead.

Property-rights creation initiatives should always pay attention to the economic sustainability of the solution advanced or desired. As long as the solutions are not supported by the various economic thresholds they are unlikely to be effective. It is not enough to design and pass legislation to change rules. To become functional such rules need the support of an entire institutional apparatus. In too many cases the reform plans are made without paying the slightest attention to that apparatus and the relevant economic variables.

Property-rights technology – the pivot of the property-rights system

The rules and incentives that give substance to property-rights systems depend on institutional and technological means of defining, monitoring and enforcing them. Understanding the means by which the various economic thresholds are dealt with in practice during the process of creating property rights is crucial for policymakers. Although the importance of property-rights technologies has been studied in the literature (Anderson and Hill, 1975, 2001; Anderson and Leal, 1991; Libecap, 1989), the full significance of the problem for attempts to create property-rights systems in international development programmes has not been sufficiently explored. The logic is inescapable: because the economic (or feasibility) threshold is critical for property-rights creation, the techniques needed or available to overcome it should be central to the effort. As a leading scholar in the field has pointed out, what is broadly defined as 'property-rights technologies' necessarily occupies a key role in our strategy of creating property rights (Yandle, 2001: 2). Understanding the nature and operation of rules and incentives is a foundational element of a development strategy, but the applicability and viability of these insights in creating institutional systems of property rights depend on the technology used.

Property-rights technologies vary from simple technical devices to complex arrangements. For example, Anderson and Hill (1975) show how the introduction of barbed wire in the American West allowed people to divide and enclose grazing land at lower cost. The process starts with a demand threshold. There was growing demand for the capability to enclose land and exclude competing grazing animals. Creative people observed the opportunity for profit. 'Inventions occur. Ergo, barbed wire is born.' But this is just a part of the story. For land to be enclosed with the help of barbed wire an environment is needed in which rights can be defined, defended and divested so that rights-holders have the incentive to search for ways to capture potential profits by installing the new technology. In other words, a critical element is omitted from the model if one does not take into account the entire institutional context. As Yandle (ibid.) puts it, 'the legal institutions that condition and affect the definition and enforcement of property rights need to be explicitly considered. For the barbed-wire story to hold, the cattlemen occupying western land must first be able to exercise the right to enclose the land'. Thus one could see a very interesting interplay of institutional and technological factors at work (Libecap, 1989: 60–64).

A contemporary example of how new technologies affect the definition of property rights involves the use of Global Positioning System (GPS) technology. Until recently, in order to document property boundaries topographic maps and traditional surveys were employed. Today, however, relatively low-cost Geographical Information Systems (GIS), including hand-held GPS devices, allow local people to create extremely accurate boundaries for property. In areas with difficult terrain, where there are few surveyors, or where financial resources are scarce, this technological shift allows people to identify, monitor and enforce property lines with great precision. A potential benefit of the technology is that resource-related conflicts may lessen as a result of increased accuracy.[1]

A different way of formulating the problem of property-rights creation technology is to start by considering that creating property rights is an (un)bundling process. As Yandle (2001: 3–8) explains, if landownership is seen as a bundle of potential rights, it is easy to see that 'lacking demand, some specialized rights might not be unbundled and traded in the market, just as some function

---

1   For information on this process, see Watermeier (2006).

within a firm awaiting growth in demand for a specialized service might remain integrated'. An unbundling depends on the existing property-rights technology available (including the 'institutional technology'). Thus the notion of unbundling may be a good vehicle for clarification of the idea of property-rights technology. The following simple list of actions illustrates the functions this technology fulfils: identify and measure the resource; defend the defined rights to the resource; enable rights to be transferred or divested; identify, assess and pre-empt threats and harm; provide information, feedback and recorded agreement, etc.

The concept of property-rights technology is an important component of the intellectual toolbox of reformers. At the same time one should not forget that it is an umbrella concept whose main function is practice-oriented. Considering it in a rigid fashion may miss the entire point. Instead, one should use it as a way of focusing attention on critical elements of the process of property-rights creation and, more precisely, on how this process implies the existence of functional instruments and techniques aimed at solving the numerous practical and operational problems intrinsic to it. Becoming aware of the crucial role of these instruments is a condition of a constructive policy approach. Instead of seeing property-rights creation as a mere fiat exercise in which 'laws' and 'rules' are promulgated in the hope that they will lead to the desired results, the notion of property-rights technology focuses our attention on the precise technical and institutional arrangements required to make those rules stick.

The crucial empirical content, relevant rules and the danger of 'slogan words'

The successful reform of property-rights institutions and the linkages between them requires an understanding of existing rules, norms and behaviour, and how these are likely to interact with new rules that are introduced. A key precondition for creating effective property rights is developing a grasp of how to ensure rules within a complex system support and reinforce each other. Accordingly, elected officials of national, state and local governments and social scientists may start by asking what rules should be changed to generate specific institutional dynamics or to solve a particular kind of problem.

Identifying the rules and understanding the operational context and implications of those rules is not easy. Authors such as Ostrom (1990, 2005) emphasise the danger of 'slogan words'. One needs to move beyond them in order to identify and describe in concrete terms how rules shape and affect the situation of concern. The task of developing a coherent understanding of how rules fit together to shape observable behaviour and outcomes is more often than not derailed – not so much by the complexity of the cases but by our own cognitive biases and confusions.

The main danger is that slogan words, such as 'privatisation', 'centralisation' or 'decentralisation', are used as substitutes for careful analysis. Instead of falling into the trap of accepting formulaic solutions, one should ask: 'What are the specific rules that we are talking about when we talk about a privatization or decentralization policy? What changes in the incentives of participants will occur if we propose a particular set of new rules versus other potential sets?' (Ostrom, 2005: 182). Indeed, the history of international development is riddled with fiascos that are the result of the belief that something called 'privatisation', once announced and implemented, will miraculously solve a host of economic and social problems.

The danger is to think and approach policy in very general and abstract terms. Even if slogan words are avoided, it is not enough to think in terms of rules and consequences. By definition rules imply a degree of generality. In working with them one could easily fall into the trap of quick-fix and universal solutions inspired by the formula 'rule X should automatically lead to behaviour Y'. For practical purposes this approach is no different from using a 'slogan word'. The solution is to recognise and understand the variety and the contextual parameters determining the application of rules and the emerging consequences. This suggests that one should have more intellectual humility, 'a substantial wariness related to the capacity of humans to design optimal systems without a substantial trial-and-error process so as to learn what works in a particular environment' (ibid.: 184).

Taking the issues that are raised in this toolbox into regular account as policy changes are proposed should help to develop an appreciation that institutional creation is a complex, evolutionary process; hence, institutional change will be similarly complex. Efforts to create secure property rights should therefore begin with as clear and complete an understanding as possible of the various legal rules (formal/informal, local/national/regional/international) that exist in a given place at a given time. Only with such an understanding will policymakers and practitioners be able to identify where on the continuum between top-down legislative fiat and bottom-up evolution any given change should be positioned.

In addition to the legal environment, reformers/practitioners must attend to the economic and sociological implications of a change to particular property rules. They should also identify other legal rules (banking, local government, conveyancing, labour, etc.) that interact with property rules to have a more accurate sense of the likely effectiveness of change. Add to this complexity the need to understand and appreciate prevailing social norms, to identify the existence or lack of property-rights technologies, both of which affect the cost of change, and one is faced with the daunting challenge of creating a realistic 'map' that will better guide policymaking in pursuit of more secure rights to property. Again, this is not to say that positive action is impossible; it is instead to caution against easy, one-size-fits-all solutions and to vigorously advocate a flexible and nuanced approach to the vital task of securing property rights for more people in the developing world.

9 CONCLUSIONS

Both the experience of failure in international development practice and the recent advances in economics and political science are changing the terms of the debate on the nature and conditions of economic development. The growing attention given to institutions and institutional change redefines not only the theoretical framework used to analyse and understand economic development but also the policies and strategies meant to generate it. In this new context, the nature of the debate over property rights and their role in development has changed. The discussion is less and less dominated by the clash between the two major 'slogan words': 'nationalisation' versus 'privatisation'. A more nuanced approach is taking shape. Creating more secure and functional property rights, and enforcing these rights, is increasingly accepted as an essential component of the developing world's economic-growth equation. A consensus is emerging that secure property rights do more than promote economic growth (an admittedly vital task): they can reduce the likelihood of resource-driven conflict, decentralise power from potentially abusive authorities and help to empower individuals. The debate is thus taking a different course now: what are the most effective policy reform strategies aimed at property-rights creation and preservation? What are the most fruitful approaches to the creation of an institutional environment conducive to efficient and flexible property-rights arrangements?

CONCLUSIONS

This study has charted some of the emerging parameters defining the answers to these crucial questions. Their basic assumption is that one needs to acknowledge and factor in the complexity of property-rights systems as well as the fact that it will take knowledge of local circumstances and local needs to identify which path to property a given society should follow at a given moment in time. Even though secure property rights provide a wide variety of benefits, we should be wary of viewing these benefits as justification for a 'one-size-fits-all' approach to property reform. This approach does not work in the regulatory sphere and is unlikely to work when it comes to providing secure, effective property rights in the developing world. The caution against over-reliance on fiat or legislation may be paralleled by balanced and realistic expectations regarding the power and limits of the evolutionary approach. In all these efforts, the costs and incentives, and the economic thresholds they create – as well as the availability of supporting institutions and technologies – should never be neglected.

The force and resilience of property-rights systems come precisely from their intrinsic flexibility – the ability to adjust and adapt to changing circumstances. An institutional environment that facilitates transactions and exchange, the free movement of goods, services and persons, is the ultimate basis of that much-needed flexibility. Overall, one needs to think of property-rights policy as a strategic process, not a blueprint-based social engineering undertaking. The complexity and uncertainty defining institutional change require us to shun the illusion of a definitive, universal answer.

We must go beyond the temptation of quick-fix solutions and the mirage of 'slogan words'. The risks are simply too high and expectations regarding property-rights policies are rising. Much more is at stake each time a developing nation undertakes property-rights policy reforms. The real danger is that the accumulated failures resulting from defective policies will lead, sooner or later, to an overall dismissal of the idea that secure property is essential for growth and human flourishing. As a consequence, this promising path to development may be abandoned. In our view, there is only one way to stop this disturbing possibility: more realistic and better informed implementation strategies.

REFERENCES

Acemoglu, D., S. Johnson and J. A. Robinson (2001), 'An African success story: Botswana', MIT Department of Economics Working Paper 01-37.

Adebayo, A. A. and P. W. Adebayo (2000), 'Sustainable housing policy and practice – reducing constraints and expanding horizons within housing delivery', *Proceedings: Strategies for Sustainable Built Environment*, 5, available at: *www.sustainablesettlement.co.za/event/SSBE/Proceedings/adebayo.pdf*.

Alden Wiley, L. (2006), 'The commons and customary law in modern times: rethinking the orthodoxies', in *Land Rights for African Development*, Washington, DC: Consultative Group on International Agricultural Research.

Anderson, S. (2005), 'Botswana: land of paradoxes', *Mercatus Policy Series*, Country Brief 1.

Anderson, T. L. and P. J. Hill (1975), 'The evolution of property rights: a study of the American West', *Journal of Law & Economics*, 18(1): 163–79.

Anderson, T. L. and P. J. Hill (2001), *The Technology of Property Rights*, Lanham, MD: Rowman and Littlefield.

Anderson, T. L. and P. J. Hill (2003), 'The evolution of property rights', in T. L. Anderson and F. S. McChesney (eds),

Property Rights: Cooperation, Conflict, and Law, Princeton, NJ: Princeton University Press, pp. 120–24.

Anderson, T. and D. Leal (1991), *Free Market Environmentalism*, Boulder, CO: Westview Press; revised edn (2001), New York: Palgrave.

Ault, D. E. and G. L. Rutman (1979), 'The development of individual rights in property in tribal Africa', *Journal of Law and Economics*, 22(1): 163–82.

Barry, N. (1998), *The Invisible Hand in Economics and Politics*, London: Institute of Economic Affairs.

Barzel, Y. (1997), *Economic Analysis of Property Rights* (2nd edn), Cambridge: Cambridge University Press.

Bickman, L. (1987), 'The function of program theory', *New Directions for Program Evaluation*, 33: 5–18.

Black's Law Dictionary (1983), Abridged 5th edn, St Paul, MN: West Publishing Co., s.v. 'Property Right'.

Blocher, J. (2006), 'Note: building on custom: land tenure policy and economic development in Ghana', *Yale Human Rights and Development Law Journal*, 9: 173.

Boettke, P., B. Hooks and P. Aligica (2004), 'The Millennium Challenge Account: property rights and entrepreneurship as the engine of development', *Public Interest Comment*, Mercatus Center at George Mason University.

Boudreaux, K. C. (2005a), 'The role of property rights as an institution: implications for development policy', Mercatus Policy Series, Policy Primer no. 2, pp. 15–16, available at: *www.mercatus.org/repository/docLib/MC_GPI_PS-property_2005_5_3.pdf*.

Boudreaux, K. C. (2005b), 'The human face of conflict: property and power in Nigeria', *San Diego International Law Journal*, 7(1): 61–102.

Boudreaux, K. C. (2006), 'The effects of property titling in Langa township, South Africa', Mercatus Policy Series, Policy Primer no. 4.

Boudreaux, K. C. (2007), 'Community-based natural resource management and poverty alleviation in Namibia', Mercatus Policy Series, Policy Primer no. 11.

Coldham, S. F. R. (1979), 'Land-tenure reform in Kenya: the limits of law', *Journal of Modern African Studies*, 17(4): 615–27.

Dam, K. W. (2006), *The Law-Growth Nexus*, Washington, DC: Brookings Institution.

De Soto, H. (2000), *The Mystery of Capital*, New York: Basic Books.

Deininger, K. (2003), *Land Policies for Growth and Poverty Reduction*, Washington, DC: World Bank and Oxford University Press.

Demsetz, H. (1967), 'Toward a theory of property rights', *American Economic Review*, 57(2): 350.

Dougan, H. (2004), 'Securing property rights in land: politics on the land frontier in postcolonial Ghana and Botswana', available at: *www.scsci2.ucsd.edu*.

Durand-Lasserve, A. (2006), 'Informal settlements and the Millennium Development Goals: global policy debates on property ownership and security of tenure', *Global Urban Development*, 2(1): 1–15.

Easterly, W. R. (2002), *The Elusive Quest for Growth: Economists' Adventures and Misadventures in the Tropics*, Cambridge, MA: MIT Press.

Easterly, W. R. (2003), 'Can foreign aid buy growth?', *Journal of Economic Perspectives*, 17: 23–48.

Eggertsson, T. (1997) 'Rethinking the theory of economic policy: some implications of the new institutionalism', in D. North (ed.), *Transforming Post-Communist Political Economies*, Washington, DC: National Resource Council, National Academy of Sciences.

Ensminger, J. E. (1997), 'Changing property rights: reconciling formal and informal rights to land in Africa', in J. N. Drobak and J. V. C. Nye (eds), *The Frontiers of the New Institutional Economics*, New York: Academic Press.

Ensminger, J. E. (2004), 'Market integration and fairness: evidence from ultimatum, dictator, and public goods experiments in East Africa', in Joseph Henrich, Robert Boyd, Samuel Bowles, Colin Camerer, Ernst Fehr and Herbert Gintis (eds), *Foundations of Human Sociality: Economic Experiments and Ethnographic Evidence from Fifteen Small-Scale Societies*, London: Oxford University Press.

Falola, T. (1999) *The History of Nigeria*, Westport, CT: Greenwood Press.

Feeny, D. (1993) 'The demand for and supply of institutional arrangements', in V. Ostrom, D. Feeny and H. Picht (eds), *Rethinking Institutional Analysis and Development*, San Francisco, CA: ICS Press.

Glaeser, E., J. Scheinkman and A. Shleifer (2003), 'The injustice of inequality', *Journal of Monetary Economics*, 50: 199–222.

Gradstein, M. (2004), 'Governance and growth', *Journal of Development Economics*, 73: 505–18.

Hansen, A. (1963), *Monetary Theory and Fiscal Policy*, New York: McGraw-Hill.

Hayek, F. A. (1944), *The Road to Serfdom*, Chicago, IL: University of Chicago Press.

Hayek, F. A. (1973), *Law, Legislation, and Liberty*, vol. 1, Chicago, IL: University of Chicago Press.

Hayek, F. A. (1974), 'The pretence of knowledge', Nobel Prize Lecture, 11 December.

Heller, M. A. (1998), 'The tragedy of the anticommons: property in the transition from Marx to markets', *Harvard Law Review*, 111(3): 621–88.

Henrich, J., R. Boyd, S. Bowles, C. Camerer, E. Fehr, H. Gintis, R. McElreath, M. Alvard, A. Barr, J. Ensminger, N. Smith, K. Henrich, F. Hill, M. Gil-White, F. W. Gurven, J. Marlowe, Q. Patton and D. Tracer (2005), 'Economic man in cross-cultural perspective: behavioral experiments in 15 small-scale societies', *Behavioral and Brain Sciences*, 29: 795–855.

Hume, D. (1978), *A Treatise of Human Nature*, Oxford: Oxford University Press.

IPRI (International Property Rights Index) (2007), *International Property Rights Index (IPRI) 2007 Report*, Washington, DC: IPRI.

Jones, B. T. B. (1999), 'Community management of natural resources in Namibia', Scandinavian Seminar College's Africa Project, SCC Africa Project no. 37.

Kagwanja, J. (2006), 'Land tenure, land reform, and the management of land and natural resources in Africa', in *Land Rights for African Development*, Washington, DC: Consultative Group on International Agricultural Research.

Knack, S. and P. Keefer (1995), 'Institutions and economic performance: cross country tests using alternative institutional measures', *Economics and Politics*, 7: 207–27.

Lesorogol, C. K. (2003), 'Transforming institutions among pastoralists: inequality and land privatization', *American Anthropologist*, 105(3): 531–42.

Li, D. D. (1996), 'A theory of ambiguous property rights in transition economies: the case of the Chinese non-state sector', *Journal of Comparative Economics*, 23: 1–19.

Libecap, G. (1989), 'Contracting for property rights', New York: Cambridge University Press.

Libecap, G. (2000), 'Contracting for property rights', Department of Economics, University of Arizona, Working Paper 7, pp. 17–18, available at: http://econ.eller.arizona.edu/downloads/working_papers/anderson3s.pdf.

Lund, C., R. Odgaard and E. Sjaastad (2006), *Land Rights and Land Conflicts in Africa: A review of issues and experiences*, Copenhagen: Danish Institute for International Studies.

Maloney, M. T. and B. Yandle (1983), 'Building markets for tradable pollution rights', in T. L. Anderson (ed.), *Water Rights: Scarce Resource Allocation, Bureaucracy, and the Environment*, San Francisco, CA: Pacific Institute for Public Policy Research, pp. 283–320.

McAuslan, P. (2006), 'Legal pluralism as a policy option: is it desirable? Is it doable?', in *Land Rights for African Development*, Washington, DC: Consultative Group on International Agricultural Research.

Netting, R. M. (1968), *The Hill Farmers of Nigeria*, Seattle: University of Washington Press.

Netting, R. M., M. P. Stone and G. Stone (1989), 'Kofyar cash cropping: choice and change in indigenous agricultural development', *Human Ecology*, 17(3): 299–319.

North, D. C. (1989), 'Institutions and economic growth: an historical introduction', *World Development*, 17: 1319–22.

North, D. C. (1990), *Institutions, Institutional Change and Economic Performance*, New York: Cambridge University Press.

North, D. C. (1993), 'Economic performance through time', Nobel Prize Lecture, 9 December, available at: http://nobelprize.org/nobel_prizes/economics/laureates/1993/north-lecture.html.

North, D. C. (1997), 'Understanding economic change', in J. M. Nelson, C. Tilley and L. Walker (eds), *Transforming Post-Communist Political Economies*, Washington, DC: National Academy Press.

North, D. C. and R. P. Thomas (1973), *The Rise of the Western World*, New York: Cambridge University Press.

Olawale Elias, T. (1962), *Nigerian Land Law and Custom*, London: Routledge and Kegan Paul.

Olson, M. (1982), *The Rise and Decline of Nations: Economic Growth, Stagflation, and Social Rigidities*, New Haven, CT: Yale University Press.

Olson, M. (1997), 'The new institutional economics: the collective choice approach to economic development', in C. Clague (ed.), *Institutions and Economic Development. Growth and Governance in Less-Developed and Post-Socialist Countries*, Baltimore, MD: Johns Hopkins University Press.

Ostrom, E. (1990), *Governing the Commons: The Evolution of Institutions for Collective Action*, Cambridge: Cambridge University Press.

Ostrom, E. (2005), *Understanding Institutional Diversity*, Princeton, NJ: Princeton University Press.

Ostrom, V. (1993), 'Opportunity, diversity and complexity', in V. Ostrom, D. Feeny and H. Picht (eds), *Rethinking Institutional Analysis and Development: Issues, Alternatives, and Choices*, San Francisco, CA: Institute for Contemporary Studies Press.

Pinckney, T. C. and P. K. Kimuyu (1994), 'Land tenure reform in East Africa: good, bad or unimportant?', *Journal of African Economies*, 3(1): 1–28.

Pipes, R. (1999), *Property and Freedom*, New York: Knopf.

Platteau, J.-P. (1996), 'The evolutionary theory of land rights as applied to sub-Saharan Africa: a critical assessment', *Development and Change*, 27: 27–86.

Platteau, J.-P. (2000), *Institutions, Social Norms, and Economic Development*, Amsterdam: Overseas Publishers Association.

Polishchuk, L. and A. Savvateev (2004), 'Spontaneous (non) emergence of property rights', *Economics of Transition*, 12(1): 103–27.

Putnam, R. (1994), *Making Democracy Work: Civic Traditions in Modern Italy*, Princeton, NJ: Princeton University Press.

Quisumbing, A., J. B. Aidoo, E. Payongayong and K. Otsuka (2001), 'Agroforestry management in Ghana', in K. Otsuka and F. Place (eds), *Land Tenure and Natural Resource Management*, Baltimore, MD, p. 55.

Rodrik, D., A. Subramanian and F. Trebbe (2004), 'Institutions rule: the primacy of institutions over geography and integration in economic development', *Journal of Economic Growth*, 9: 131–65.

Rossi, P. (2004), *Evaluation*, London: Sage Publications.

Sanjak, J. (2004), 'Commentary and reaction to theme paper/ legal and regulatory requirements for effective rural financial markets', Paper presented at Paving the Way Forward for

Rural Finance, Conference on Best Practices, available at: *www.basis.wisc.edu/rfc/documents/theme_legal_r1.pdf*.

Smith, A. (1976), *An Inquiry into the Nature and Causes of the Wealth of Nations*, New York: Oxford University Press.

Sonin, K. (2002), 'Why the rich may favor poor protection of property rights', William Davidson Working Paper 544 (December).

USAID (2007), 'Policy reform lessons learned: a review of economic growth related policy reform activities in developing countries', Washington, DC: USAID.

Verdery, K. (2003), *The Vanishing Hectare*, Ithaca, NY: Cornell University Press.

Watermeier, N. (2006), 'Creating and using geo-referenced field boundaries', Ohio Geospatial Program for Agriculture and Natural Resources, available at: http://geospatial.osu.edu/resources/GeorefBoundaries.pdf.

Weingast, B. R. (1995), 'The economic role of political institutions: market-preserving federalism and economic development', *Journal of Law, Economics, and Organization*, 11: 1–31.

Williams, D. C. (1992), 'Measuring the impact of land reform policy in Nigeria', *Journal of Modern African Studies*, 30: 587.

Yandle, B. (2001), 'Legal foundations for evolving property rights technologies', in T. L. Anderson and P. J. Hill (eds), *The Technology of Property Rights*, Lanham, MD: Rowman and Littlefield.

Zak, P. J. (2002), 'Institutions, property rights and growth', *Louvain Economic Review*, 68: 55–73.

Zhang, X. (2005), 'Asymmetric property rights in China's economic growth', Paper presented at the Annual American Economics Association Meetings, Boston, MA, 6–8 January.

ABOUT THE IEA

The Institute is a research and educational charity (No. CC 235 351), limited by guarantee. Its mission is to improve understanding of the fundamental institutions of a free society by analysing and expounding the role of markets in solving economic and social problems.

The IEA achieves its mission by:

- a high-quality publishing programme
- conferences, seminars, lectures and other events
- outreach to school and college students
- brokering media introductions and appearances

The IEA, which was established in 1955 by the late Sir Antony Fisher, is an educational charity, not a political organisation. It is independent of any political party or group and does not carry on activities intended to affect support for any political party or candidate in any election or referendum, or at any other time. It is financed by sales of publications, conference fees and voluntary donations.

In addition to its main series of publications the IEA also publishes a quarterly journal, *Economic Affairs*.

The IEA is aided in its work by a distinguished international Academic Advisory Council and an eminent panel of Honorary Fellows. Together with other academics, they review prospective IEA publications, their comments being passed on anonymously to authors. All IEA papers are therefore subject to the same rigorous independent refereeing process as used by leading academic journals.

IEA publications enjoy widespread classroom use and course adoptions in schools and universities. They are also sold throughout the world and often translated/reprinted.

Since 1974 the IEA has helped to create a worldwide network of 100 similar institutions in over 70 countries. They are all independent but share the IEA's mission.

Views expressed in the IEA's publications are those of the authors, not those of the Institute (which has no corporate view), its Managing Trustees, Academic Advisory Council members or senior staff.

Members of the Institute's Academic Advisory Council, Honorary Fellows, Trustees and Staff are listed on the following page.

The Institute gratefully acknowledges financial support for its publications programme and other work from a generous benefaction by the late Alec and Beryl Warren.

The Institute of Economic Affairs
2 Lord North Street, Westminster, London SW1P 3LB
Tel: 020 7799 8900
Fax: 020 7799 2137
Email: iea@iea.org.uk
Internet: iea.org.uk

Director General & Ralph Harris Fellow   John Blundell

Editorial Director   Professor Philip Booth

Managing Trustees

Chairman: Professor D R Myddelton
Kevin Bell
Robert Boyd
Michael Fisher
Michael Hintze
Malcolm McAlpine

Professor Patrick Minford
Professor Martin Ricketts
Professor J R Shackleton
Linda Whetstone

Academic Advisory Council

Chairman: Professor Martin Ricketts
Graham Bannock
Professor Norman Barry
Dr Roger Bate
Professor Alberto Benegas-Lynch, Jr
Professor Donald J Boudreaux
Professor John Burton
Professor Forrest Capie
Professor Steven N S Cheung
Professor Tim Congdon
Professor N F R Crafts
Professor David de Meza
Professor Kevin Dowd
Professor Richard A Epstein
Nigel Essex
Professor David Greenaway
Dr Ingrid A Gregg
Walter E Grinder
Professor Steve H Hanke
Professor Keith Hartley
Professor David Henderson
Professor Peter M Jackson
Dr Jerry Jordan
Dr Lynne Kiesling
Professor Daniel B Klein

Professor Stephen C Littlechild
Dr Eileen Marshall
Professor Antonio Martino
Dr Anja Merz
Professor Julian Morris
Paul Ormerod
Professor David Parker
Dr Mark Pennington
Professor Victoria Curzon Price
Professor Colin Robinson
Professor Charles K Rowley
Professor Pascal Salin
Dr Razeen Sally
Professor Pedro Schwartz
Jane S Shaw
Professor W Stanley Siebert
Dr Elaine Sternberg
Professor James Tooley
Professor Nicola Tynan
Professor Roland Vaubel
Professor Lawrence H White
Professor Walter E Williams
Professor Geoffrey E Wood

Honorary Fellows

Professor Armen A Alchian
Professor Michael Beenstock
Sir Samuel Brittan
Professor James M Buchanan
Professor Ronald H Coase
Dr R M Hartwell
Professor Terence W Hutchison
Professor David Laidler
Professor Dennis S Lees

Professor Chiaki Nishiyama
Professor Sir Alan Peacock
Professor Ben Roberts
Professor Anna J Schwartz
Professor Vernon L Smith
Professor Gordon Tullock
Professor Sir Alan Walters
Professor Basil S Yamey

Other papers recently published by the IEA include:

WHO, What and Why?
Transnational Government, Legitimacy and the World Health Organization
Roger Scruton
Occasional Paper 113; ISBN 0 255 36487 3; £8.00

The World Turned Rightside Up
A New Trading Agenda for the Age of Globalisation
John C. Hulsman
Occasional Paper 114; ISBN 0 255 36495 4; £8.00

The Representation of Business in English Literature
Introduced and edited by Arthur Pollard
Readings 53; ISBN 0 255 36491 1; £12.00

Anti-Liberalism 2000
The Rise of New Millennium Collectivism
David Henderson
Occasional Paper 115; ISBN 0 255 36497 0; £7.50

Capitalism, Morality and Markets
Brian Griffiths, Robert A. Sirico, Norman Barry & Frank Field
Readings 54; ISBN 0 255 36496 2; £7.50

A Conversation with Harris and Seldon
Ralph Harris & Arthur Seldon
Occasional Paper 116; ISBN 0 255 36498 9; £7.50

Malaria and the DDT Story
Richard Tren & Roger Bate
Occasional Paper 117; ISBN 0 255 36499 7; £10.00

A Plea to Economists Who Favour Liberty: Assist the Everyman
Daniel B. Klein
Occasional Paper 118; ISBN 0 255 36501 2; £10.00

The Changing Fortunes of Economic Liberalism
Yesterday, Today and Tomorrow
David Henderson
Occasional Paper 105 (new edition); ISBN 0 255 36520 9; £12.50

The Global Education Industry
Lessons from Private Education in Developing Countries
James Tooley
Hobart Paper 141 (new edition); ISBN 0 255 36503 9; £12.50

Saving Our Streams
The Role of the Anglers' Conservation Association in Protecting English and Welsh Rivers
Roger Bate
Research Monograph 53; ISBN 0 255 36494 6; £10.00

Better Off Out?
The Benefits or Costs of EU Membership
Brian Hindley & Martin Howe
Occasional Paper 99 (new edition); ISBN 0 255 36502 0; £10.00

Buckingham at 25
Freeing the Universities from State Control
Edited by James Tooley
Readings 55; ISBN 0 255 36512 8; £15.00

Lectures on Regulatory and Competition Policy
Irwin M. Stelzer
Occasional Paper 120; ISBN 0 255 36511 x; £12.50

Misguided Virtue
False Notions of Corporate Social Responsibility
David Henderson
Hobart Paper 142; ISBN 0 255 36510 1; £12.50

HIV and Aids in Schools
The Political Economy of Pressure Groups and Miseducation
Barrie Craven, Pauline Dixon, Gordon Stewart & James Tooley
Occasional Paper 121; ISBN 0 255 36522 5; £10.00

The Road to Serfdom
The Reader's Digest *condensed version*
Friedrich A. Hayek
Occasional Paper 122; ISBN 0 255 36530 6; £7.50

Bastiat's *The Law*
Introduction by Norman Barry
Occasional Paper 123; ISBN 0 255 36509 8; £7.50

A Globalist Manifesto for Public Policy
Charles Calomiris
Occasional Paper 124; ISBN 0 255 36525 X; £7.50

Euthanasia for Death Duties
Putting Inheritance Tax Out of Its Misery
Barry Bracewell-Milnes
Research Monograph 54; ISBN 0 255 36513 6; £10.00

Liberating the Land
The Case for Private Land-use Planning
Mark Pennington
Hobart Paper 143; ISBN 0 255 36508 X; £10.00

IEA Yearbook of Government Performance 2002/2003
Edited by Peter Warburton
Yearbook 1; ISBN 0 255 36532 2; £15.00

Britain's Relative Economic Performance, 1870–1999
Nicholas Crafts
Research Monograph 55; ISBN 0 255 36524 1; £10.00

Should We Have Faith in Central Banks?
Otmar Issing
Occasional Paper 125; ISBN 0 255 36528 4; £7.50

The Dilemma of Democracy
Arthur Seldon
Hobart Paper 136 (reissue); ISBN 0 255 36536 5; £10.00

Capital Controls: a 'Cure' Worse Than the Problem?
Forrest Capie
Research Monograph 56; ISBN 0 255 36506 3; £10.00

The Poverty of 'Development Economics'
Deepak Lal
Hobart Paper 144 (reissue); ISBN 0 255 36519 5; £15.00

Should Britain Join the Euro?
The Chancellor's Five Tests Examined
Patrick Minford
Occasional Paper 126; ISBN 0 255 36527 6; £7.50

Post-Communist Transition: Some Lessons
Leszek Balcerowicz
Occasional Paper 127; ISBN 0 255 36533 0; £7.50

A Tribute to Peter Bauer
John Blundell et al.
Occasional Paper 128; ISBN 0 255 36531 4; £10.00

Employment Tribunals
Their Growth and the Case for Radical Reform
J. R. Shackleton
Hobart Paper 145; ISBN 0 255 36515 2; £10.00

Fifty Economic Fallacies Exposed
Geoffrey E. Wood
Occasional Paper 129; ISBN 0 255 36518 7; £12.50

A Market in Airport Slots
Keith Boyfield (editor), David Starkie, Tom Bass & Barry Humphreys
Readings 56; ISBN 0 255 36505 5; £10.00

Money, Inflation and the Constitutional Position of the Central Bank
Milton Friedman & Charles A. E. Goodhart
Readings 57; ISBN 0 255 36538 1; £10.00

railway.com
Parallels between the Early British Railways and the ICT Revolution
Robert C. B. Miller
Research Monograph 57; ISBN 0 255 36534 9; £12.50

The Regulation of Financial Markets
Edited by Philip Booth & David Currie
Readings 58; ISBN 0 255 36551 9; £12.50

Climate Alarmism Reconsidered
Robert L. Bradley Jr
Hobart Paper 146; ISBN 0 255 36541 1; £12.50

Government Failure: E. G. West on Education
Edited by James Tooley & James Stanfield
Occasional Paper 130; ISBN 0 255 36552 7; £12.50

Corporate Governance: Accountability in the Marketplace
Elaine Sternberg
Second edition
Hobart Paper 147; ISBN 0 255 36542 X; £12.50

The Land Use Planning System
Evaluating Options for Reform
John Corkindale
Hobart Paper 148; ISBN 0 255 36550 0; £10.00

Economy and Virtue
Essays on the Theme of Markets and Morality
Edited by Dennis O'Keeffe
Readings 59; ISBN 0 255 36504 7; £12.50

Free Markets Under Siege
Cartels, Politics and Social Welfare
Richard A. Epstein
Occasional Paper 132; ISBN 0 255 36553 5; £10.00

Unshackling Accountants
D. R. Myddelton
Hobart Paper 149; ISBN 0 255 36559 4; £12.50

The Euro as Politics
Pedro Schwartz
Research Monograph 58; ISBN 0 255 36535 7; £12.50

Pricing Our Roads
Vision and Reality
Stephen Glaister & Daniel J. Graham
Research Monograph 59; ISBN 0 255 36562 4; £10.00

The Role of Business in the Modern World
Progress, Pressures, and Prospects for the Market Economy
David Henderson
Hobart Paper 150; ISBN 0 255 36548 9; £12.50

Public Service Broadcasting Without the BBC?
Alan Peacock
Occasional Paper 133; ISBN 0 255 36565 9; £10.00

The ECB and the Euro: the First Five Years
Otmar Issing
Occasional Paper 134; ISBN 0 255 36555 1; £10.00

Towards a Liberal Utopia?
Edited by Philip Booth
Hobart Paperback 32; ISBN 0 255 36563 2; £15.00

The Way Out of the Pensions Quagmire
Philip Booth & Deborah Cooper
Research Monograph 60; ISBN 0 255 36517 9; £12.50

Black Wednesday
A Re-examination of Britain's Experience in the Exchange Rate Mechanism
Alan Budd
Occasional Paper 135; ISBN 0 255 36566 7; £7.50

Crime: Economic Incentives and Social Networks
Paul Ormerod
Hobart Paper 151; ISBN 0 255 36554 3; £10.00

The Road to Serfdom *with* **The Intellectuals and Socialism**
Friedrich A. Hayek
Occasional Paper 136; ISBN 0 255 36576 4; £10.00

Money and Asset Prices in Boom and Bust
Tim Congdon
Hobart Paper 152; ISBN 0 255 36570 5; £10.00

The Dangers of Bus Re-regulation
and Other Perspectives on Markets in Transport
John Hibbs et al.
Occasional Paper 137; ISBN 0 255 36572 1; £10.00

The New Rural Economy
Change, Dynamism and Government Policy
Berkeley Hill et al.
Occasional Paper 138; ISBN 0 255 36546 2; £15.00

The Benefits of Tax Competition
Richard Teather
Hobart Paper 153; ISBN 0 255 36569 1; £12.50

Wheels of Fortune
Self-funding Infrastructure and the Free Market Case for a Land Tax
Fred Harrison
Hobart Paper 154; ISBN 0 255 36589 6; £12.50

Were 364 Economists All Wrong?
Edited by Philip Booth
Readings 60; ISBN 978 0 255 36588 8; £10.00

Europe After the 'No' Votes
Mapping a New Economic Path
Patrick A. Messerlin
Occasional Paper 139; ISBN 978 0 255 36580 2; £10.00

The Railways, the Market and the Government
John Hibbs et al.
Readings 61; ISBN 978 0 255 36567 3; £12.50

Corruption: The World's Big C
Cases, Causes, Consequences, Cures
Ian Senior
Research Monograph 61; ISBN 978 0 255 36571 0; £12.50

Choice and the End of Social Housing
Peter King
Hobart Paper 155; ISBN 978 0 255 36568 0; £10.00

Sir Humphrey's Legacy
Facing Up to the Cost of Public Sector Pensions
Neil Record
Hobart Paper 156; ISBN 978 0 255 36578 9; £10.00

The Economics of Law
Cento Veljanovski
Second edition
Hobart Paper 157; ISBN 978 0 255 36561 1; £12.50

Living with Leviathan
Public Spending, Taxes and Economic Performance
David B. Smith
Hobart Paper 158; ISBN 978 0 255 36579 6; £12.50

The Vote Motive
Gordon Tullock
New edition
Hobart Paperback 33; ISBN 978 0 255 36577 2; £10.00

Waging the War of Ideas
John Blundell
Third edition
Occasional Paper 131; ISBN 978 0 255 36606 9; £12.50

The War Between the State and the Family
How Government Divides and Impoverishes
Patricia Morgan
Hobart Paper 159; ISBN 978 0 255 36596 3; £10.00

Capitalism – A Condensed Version
Arthur Seldon
Occasional Paper 140; ISBN 978 0 255 36598 7; £7.50

Catholic Social Teaching and the Market Economy
Edited by Philip Booth
Hobart Paperback 34; ISBN 978 0 255 36581 9; £15.00

Adam Smith – A Primer
Eamonn Butler
Occasional Paper 141; ISBN 978 0 255 36608 3; £7.50

Happiness, Economics and Public Policy
Helen Johns & Paul Ormerod
Research Monograph 62; ISBN 978 0 255 36600 7; £10.00

They Meant Well
Government Project Disasters
D. R. Myddelton
Hobart Paper 160; ISBN 978 0 255 36601 4; £12.50

Rescuing Social Capital from Social Democracy
John Meadowcroft & Mark Pennington
Hobart Paper 161; ISBN 978 0 255 36592 5; £10.00

All the listed IEA papers, including those that are out of print, can be downloaded from www.iea.org.uk. Purchases can also be made through the website. To order copies of currently available IEA papers, or to enquire about availability, please contact:

Gazelle
IEA orders
FREEPOST RLYS-EAHU-YSCZ
White Cross Mills
Hightown
Lancaster LA1 4XS

Tel: 01524 68765
Fax: 01524 63232
Email: sales@gazellebooks.co.uk

The IEA also offers a subscription service to its publications. For a single annual payment, currently £42.00 in the UK, you will receive every monograph the IEA publishes during the course of a year and discounts on our extensive back catalogue. For more information, please contact:

Adam Myers
Subscriptions
The Institute of Economic Affairs
2 Lord North Street
London SW1P 3LB

Tel: 020 7799 8920
Fax: 020 7799 2137
Website: www.iea.org.uk